Additional Advance praise for

A BOOK OF COMMON POWl

"Dizzying...makes for exciting reading and contemplation. The surprises jump from sentence to sentence leaving the reader exhilarated and mentally and spiritually breathless...Her style of writing jumps off the page into your mind like speeding bullets — there to take fruit and hide and pop up again when least expected."
Anne Benedict, mother, teacher
Inner-city community organizer

"Donna Schaper writes from rich life experience which she shares with biblical grounding, depth of feeling, and with a freshness of metaphor. She shares her own sound insights into life itself which she embraces even as she struggles with the rat race of upper mobility, the demands and love of her three children, the hypocrisy of religious institutions, and the need to be alone. Her observations are a special gift. She strikes chords that will resonate with men and women who are seeking to be faithful."
George W. Webber, Ph.D.
New York Theological Seminary

"[Schaper's] words often rush passionately and at other moments linger compassionately, leaving the reader breathless but never bored."
May S. Lord
Winner of the Compañera Award for Sanctuary work

"Not a how-to book, nor a guide book — but simply a "what is" book. We are invited along on Donna's honest, relentless and thorough examination of her own life and thus all of our lives too. We learn as she learns. She said, "I write to clarify, to see what is so and what isn't." I want to thank her for that edifying clarity — for exposing the truth when so many others are afraid or just don't have the time."
Marianna Houston, playwright and mother
Co-author of *Mama Drama*

A BOOK of COMMON POWER

Narratives against the current

by donna schaper

San Diego, California

LuraMedia ™

© Copyright 1989 LuraMedia
San Diego, California
International Copyright Secured
Publisher's Catalog Number LM-617
Printed and Bound in the United States of America

Cover design by Carol Jeanotilla, Denver, Colorado.

LuraMedia
7060 Miramar Road, Suite 104
San Diego, CA 92121

Library of Congress Cataloging-in-Publication Data

Schaper, Donna.
    A book of common power : narratives against the current / by
    Donna Schaper.
        p. cm.
    Bibliography: p.
    ISBN 0-931055-67-9
    1. Church work with the poor. 2. Church and social problems.
3. Christian life—1960–   4. Christianity—20th century.
5. Schaper, Donna. I. Title.
BV639.P6S29 1989
261.8—dc20   89-12222
                                                                 CIP

The Scripture quotations are from THE REVISED STANDARD VERSION OF THE
BIBLE, copyright 1946, 1952, 1971 by the Division of Christian Education of the
National Council of the Churches of Christ in the U.S.A. Used by permission.

To Cassie Nutter
who opened my eyes
to the strength of ordinary people.

ACKNOWLEDGMENTS

I want to thank my husband, Warren, and my children, Isaac, Katie, and Jacob, for releasing me to the second floor where I was able, often enough, to write without interruption. I also thank my parish, the First Congregational Church in Riverhead, for their many encouragements. My friend Ann Marie Coleman has been a constant source of encouragement as well, as have many others, who have said yes to the writing down of these stories of hope. John McKnight's writings have influenced these in many ways, and Cassie Nutter, as my "trainer" in the Office of Economic Opportunity in 1970, required me to learn more than I have yet absorbed about the strengths of ordinary people. Of all my mentors in community organizing, she remains the best.

contents

1
the pains
of various passions

BURNOUT

the pains
of various passions

BURNOUT

IT USED TO matter to me that I couldn't track down the correct spelling of the Japanese word *Kolor*, the meaning of which I'm told is the fear that your penis is shrinking. It's such an interesting word. Since my burnout, I am less likely to care precisely. I have neither the time nor the will.

A phrase with as much color as *Kolor* should be invented if it doesn't already exist, and on that wish I will hinge my laziness. There should be a companion word for women, which English possibly has in menopause. The gradual loss of fertility is not just worrisome; it also announces itself in famous hot flashes and bitchiness. We fear mentally and experience physically our loss. I never heard of a penis actually shrinking. Maybe we women are better off because something actually happens and we become different. I don't know yet.

My familiarity with *Kolor* is altogether spiritual: I know about fear. Burnout is 90 percent fear and the rest circumstance. I not only lost my energy and will for a time; I also worried so much that they were gone that I lost light and lived in darkness. My burnout was more my brownout. You get to keep on with some of what you were doing. You can move around. You can still talk. You can touch. But it all feels wrong. When the lights go out, body or soul, there is a waiting that joins worrying, the combination of which postpones living.

I groped around. I was profoundly aware that it used to be different. I used to be able to tolerate the listlessness of the late afternoons; then I had to sleep through them or fidget. I was formerly glad if an old friend called; then I wondered what she wanted, when she wanted it. I calculated burden. Could I bear it? How could I get out of it?

My past energy took on a glow as though I'd never been tired or frustrated before that winter when it came. I began to notice the indifferences. A lot that used to matter didn't any more. A clean house, dry cleaning retrieved. Some days even children's runny noses. I cared most about the day's capacity to leave me alone. When would I be free to sit? When would all the things I used to love stop bothering me? When could my loneliness be alone?

I didn't give the name burnout to these episodes of indifference until long after they began. My friends were quick (quack?) to supply that diagnosis, but I despised the word and wanted no part of it. It was a loan from the world of machines, and I had a habit of spraying eloquence on it whenever it appeared. Humans and machines are different, therefore our woes deserve suitable language instead of false metaphor. By the time of my burnout, however, I no longer fiddled with the meaning or the spelling of words.

I felt like I had been plugged in much too long. My engine couldn't start without jumper-cables. The part of me that was machine-like was sputtering. The simple seemed so hard. I could no more make the same trip on the same fuel as I had in the golden before than I could light a fire without a match. I feared that my energy was shrinking, and it was.

The times didn't help. I was facing enough political defeat to last a lifetime. Peace, civil rights, feminism, the works — all had Ronald Reagan for president so that my normal seismic alienation jumped off the charts. Pundits declared that the smoke of mesquite had replaced tear gas, that dining now took the place of demonstrations, that menus were the new manifestos. I nodded, beyond shame. The words ''system-bashing'' were turning to dust in my mouth. I needed nourishment so badly that I hardly cared not to be notified of the next civil disobedience. I cared for food the way I used to care for justice: passionately, carefully, aesthetically. I wanted so badly to be fed rather than to feed. For months I refused anything but the food section of the paper. I didn't want to know any more.

My friends both did and didn't help. They ignored much of my pain because it was a reminder of their own. When they did touch it, they did so gently, beautifully. Burnout has proven to be my best invitation to join the human race, and my friends issued it. They weren't surprised by my pessimism. They did not shrink from my despair. Instead they pointed to the spot in their own hearts where these demons lay. And then they continued to discuss their last or next trip to Martinique, as though I only appeared to be dying inside.

Their ability to see beyond the ditch in which I was stuck became my own, but not until much of the rubber was worn off the tires in futile efforts to grind loose. Next time I go through all this — and now I know there will be a next time — I intend to sit. To plop. To not pretend.

Burnout is a part of living, not a detour. It is the main road, almost as natural as downshifting the car when the hills are steeper. Better words should be invented for it, like creative dislocation or wandering or shift or change or homelessness. Even transition would do, pausing to go around a curve, slowing down out of respect for its curvedness. Menopause and *Kolor* are too sexual to contain the all of it. The fact that big systems love high energy should not permit them to control language in such a way as to insult lower energies. This prejudice is not fair. Its injustice is in the alienation of most of life which is not fast but rather slow lane. It offends the ordinary courage of those of us who do manage to get our engines started after long muddy times when the fear to even try a start is great.

The time of my wandering had two beginnings. One was political; the other was personal. I'm quite convinced in retrospect that the political origin was a stop at Seneca Falls for the Women's Peace Encampment in the summer of 1983. We were moving to Chicago from Massachusetts. We stopped along the way and most of my political faith never quite got started again.

The Seneca Women's Peace Encampment to me was all symbol and picture. It reminded me of those weddings where the photographer so dominates that the vows are lost in the shutter. Or of the drawings by children which we proudly display on our refrigerators. All color. No depth. No shadow. These drawings are fine if done by eight year olds. They tell less of a story when composed by adults.

The innocence of the event to which I had looked forward greatly was marked at the gate by pillowcases on which grown women drew either their dreams or their nightmares. These flaws took the place of the national symbol. Puppets promenaded. People wore costumes and painted their faces. A large condom was draped over an even larger toy missile.

More evidence for the playfulness of the event I can't imagine. Even the conversation had a childish tone. Do we have to wear shirts? Should women touch each other in public? Should men be allowed inside the camp?

What will happen when we climb over their fence?

The people in the town of Romulus, New York, responded at a similar level, accusing the protesters of sick sex while proudly wearing OUI and PENTHOUSE T-shirts. I thought the local who declared his preference for nuclear war over relations with what he called a dyke particularly obnoxious. Who wanted him anyway?

Even the widely publicized momentary reconciliations had an adolescent flavor. So what if a national guardsman gives thirsty protesters a can of soda? As symbol, it too is sweet, sweet, sweet, implying the absurdity that success at interpersonal relationships has an effect on geopolitics.

At Seneca, protest and patriotism behaved like American twins, both trying to outdo each other in vying for the affection of their heritage and channel two. Here the twins of sentimentalism and violence squabbled and abused the symbols they shared.

There's probably no reason Seneca should have been any different than the rest of America. No reason but my hope that it might.

Both the women's movement and the peace movement here resembled that America which is a spoiled child desperately in need of maturing if peace or justice are to be established. The only difference between the innocence of the protesters and the innocence of the patriots is that the patriots have power. They have bombs. Maybe only children can stop other children. But I think not. I fear that it is going to take adults. Adults who spend their money on organization rather than summer camps. Adults who figure out how to get a hold of power and use it.

If the issue was just the symbol of bombs, then we could climb over symbolic fences and plant symbolic seeds. The bomb is no symbol. The toys the boys are playing with are real. If the ''girls'' want them to stop, they better find something real like power with which to stop them. If we want to use symbols, fine. They're actually more interesting than power and votes, but it is important to back the symbols up with some reality every now and then. Otherwise the symbols offend hope.

The women at Grenham Common in England are not known for naughty poses in front of naughty cameras. Their presence is making NATO look naughty, not their movement. They make women look like the serious creatures we are and not silly.

Like I said before, my friends helped me by seeing what I couldn't see. Among my most treasured possessions is a letter from a friend in Ohio who went to the same Seneca encampment and saw a totally different event. Her letter disagreeing with my inter-pretation required a revision of my revulsion at events there. Somehow the revision never reached my hope. It was first offended, and then it started to disappear. I spent most of my burnout time wondering if there was any reason to hope for peace, to believe in women, to practice citizenship. These all seemed thin reeds. For the first time in my life the cynics seemed right and the dreamers wrong.

Overlapping this political dismay was the birth of my first son eight weeks before the arrival at the Seneca Peace Encampment. That number eight explains a lot of my alienation from the anger of the other protesters.

I couldn't understand why all those women didn't stop the protest long enough to praise the ten pounds of new flesh which was glued to my breast. Their words seemed so abstract and Isaac's gurgles so concrete. After birth and the responsibility for new life, I never quite recovered my earlier capacity for the abstract. I wanted peace much less than that my son not be killed in a war. Caring for the faceless seemed noble but impossible.

Now I see politics as neither the earlier caring for the nameless ''other,'' nor the burnout of not being able to care, but rather the vehicle through which I protect my young. That transition was slow in coming, but now I can stand to read my mail again. I can march in demonstrations and get my congressperson on the phone. I am free again to watch the nightly news.

But I have to remember how much motherhood depoliticized me, how urgent the claim of my newborn was, how distant everything else became. I had to reevaluate all my pre-Mom politics. They seemed so shallow now.

The marriage of these two circumstances, my first baby and the new political depression, snuffed me out. I wandered in the dark, doing the best I could on my new but difficult job. The main sense I could make of it all was to carry my new baby with me wherever I went. Sometimes lugging him seemed like all the good I could do in the world. Isaac was the best bodyguard I could have as we traveled together in Chicago, him in the snuggli, me wanting to be there. It took more courage than I had to walk without hope into those neighborhoods. I kept walking but felt like I was on automatic pilot most of the time, doing the same kind of work I'd always done but without vision. The grooves were in place and so I walked in them.

I don't know yet how the all maleness of my new work situation affected all this sadness. It may have been both cause and effect, with Seneca borrowed only for symbolism. Before this time when men refused to feed or care for me, I knew enough not to be bothered. But somehow here I continued in a sleazy hope: It was impossible for men to be consistently oblivious. Surely the soul vision of their colleague and comrade was cause to care. But their attitude was much more sanguine. The struggle in the city is inevitable. Strong men have fainted before it. So why not weakened women?

These circumstances accounted for 10 percent of my burnout. The remainder was well-tutored fear. That, and my track record. By the time of my shame I had quite a track record. People counted on me for their hope. I was more a nourisher than a feeder. My success at "career" was secondary to some sense of success as a person. I had enjoyed one of those floating homes where there were always a few more for dinner, a couple of good letters in the mailbox, a phone that had to be taken off the hook a couple of times a day. I had and have country and city places where I am always welcome.

I had good friends. All my moving had left me with a national community; my work had left me with a million occasions to stay connected. I felt crucial to many communities. The idea of showing these people my scared face was alarming.

The first fear was the loss of my track record as friend; the second fear was I'd lose my friends. Surely they couldn't like me for me. They liked me for my hope. If I didn't bring it with me when I went to their homes, they'd probably throw me out. The arrival of these fears that my life was changing, and had already changed, that I was no longer the person I used to be, that even my track record was in jeopardy, and the accompanying terror that maybe these were not friends at all, threw me for quite a loop. Easily 90 percent of my dislocation was these circulating, oscillating fears. I wasn't what I used to be, if I ever was that, and maybe I'd never be it again, whatever it was.

I was unhinged.

One road out proved to be my thoughts about this whole business of track record. I needed context badly. Was I the only person ever thrown off the horse of living?

Perhaps you know my friend John. John has a track record eighty feet long. They have to add new typewriter ribbon every time they do his résumé.

He was popular in high school and popular in college. He was always invited, always consulted, and never lacked employment or money. If he did have a drink or two, he turned silly rather than morbid. If ever he feared for his soul, it didn't take long. His insides were not as well-dressed as his outsides, and there simply wasn't much to say. When his best friend died young of cancer, he cried at the funeral a few respectable tears. John never wept. After that, he had no reason.

Politics and pearls describe Sandra. She is one of the women on whom the inheritance of the women's movement fell. She is female and feminist. By the time she married her first lawyer, her kitchen was thoroughly modernized and the debt was paid off. She drove a high-priced car into which her son's high-priced car seat slid. She sat on many boards which each in their own way guaranteed the rights of women, although Sandra had never even met any of the people these boards served. She will return in a few years to her job at the bank. Right before her mother dies she'll be sure to put her in a high-quality nursing home. Sandra doesn't cry much either, only when her husband gives her a hard time, and then the tears are globules of frustration. Sandra doesn't like being out of control which is why she stopped feeling much for her son when he became a teenager. John and Sandra can be counted on never to do much harm. They can also be counted on never to do much good. They know too little of trouble.

A broken back kept Sam out of the army, out of college, and out of young male company. His parents, who cared for him until he was thirty, were on the verge of placing him in an adult home when Sam entered a sheltered workshop. There he assembled children's blocks into packages, made the coffee, and organized an after-work scrabble game. The scrabble kept five other guys plus him in good spirits. Good laughs. Good stories.

Sam did move to the adult home but only had to sleep there. The fraternity of the scrabble board kept him out late every night. He died young, in severe pain at the end. But not before his own disability enabled others.

Susan took care of her grandchildren. She and her husband were fifty-nine when the children arrived. Her daughter died at thirty-seven of breast cancer. Every time you asked Susan how it was going she shrugged her shoulders. You'd have to push her to find the meaning. Eventually she'd say that she had no choice. There was nothing else to do. Everybody said Susan was good at rising to occasions, especially the children, each of whom remember how much work they had to do at an early age. The eleven year old remembers being taught how to grocery shop and having a front and back basket on his bike. The nine year old, now a grown man, reports, and I quote from a recent conversation, ''Before Mom died

I never felt needed. Living with Grandma, I felt needed all the time.'' One of the consequences of trouble is the requirement that everyone make a contribution.

Each of these four people has a track record, but only two would bother to use it. John and Sandra are dependent on their track records; they are the kind of people who find a missing promotion a major disaster. They are as controlled by their success, it seems to me, as Sam and Susan are controlled by their trouble.

This gets us to the business of track records, which is almost as interesting a concept as burnout. Track record means running around while measuring speed and distance. Performances. Not much time for a back operation not to work or a daughter with young children to die. It is also individual, alone and unfettered. Not much chance to cooperate, or receive, or hesitate, or seek another's opinion. Not much need for another; in fact another would just get in the way. Worse, a baby or pregnancy or an aging parent. Imagine having to run the track with a dependent, an impediment, a handicap as it were.

A track record is probably a very good thing to have in a track race when the point is running and running well, if the point is an ever-growing penis. Where the point is getting from here to there as fast as possible.

It is a terrible thing when the subject is life. The word is not just suspicious; it is frightening. It sets up the wrong standard. Imagine wasting your whole life playing the notes to the wrong music, or driving in California using a New York map, or making pancakes using a cookie recipe. Setting up the wrong standard can be a frightening thing. The fear is in wasted life, in years spent dancing to the wrong drummer.

John and Sandra will always be elected homecoming queen, and president of the PTA, and senator by Sam and Susan because they will look like the kind of people we all want to be. In this culture we set up and maintain the false standard, the track record of success. Sam and Susan by their silence and their votes are as much a part of that system as John and Sandra.

They will elect John and Sandra rather than each other because they watch television, and because they read books and magazines, and because they believe the standards the false bearers wave. They will elect John and Sandra because the Bible and its story of Jesus' track record impresses them less than what advertising tells them.

They will tolerate John and Sandra as their bosses because the story of Jesus makes less noise than the story of billboards. Oddly the story of Jesus makes less noise because it is told by a slow runner, a quiet one, by a Sam and Susan type rather than a John and Sandra type.

If John and Sandra were in charge of the Jesus story, they'd get it on prime time. As long as Sam and Susan are in charge of the Jesus story, it will go slowly. It will be as quiet and humble in its presentation as it is in its substance. It will not be like Sandra, in control all the time or even a little of the time. It will not be like John who can't weep.

Jesus' track record was the wound in his side. When he came back to his disciples and they asked him for reason to accept him as Messiah, he put their hands in the wound. He used the wounds as evidence of who he was. They were his credentials. Not a résumé. Not a string of appropriately spaced successes, each confirming the last ability. No evidence of strength or energy. Not dressed for success.

He took their hands and guided them to the place where he was hurt. I know only a little of what this means for the John or Sandra in me. I fear a rejection of ability and capability. I refuse to believe that God enjoys a good track meet any less than you or I. The God of biblical faith exults in human prowess and, I imagine, is as glued to the TV set as we are during the Olympics, glad for the excellence of body, or sharpness of mind, or deftness in the arts of community.

Human abilities are not put down by God but rather elevated to praise. They are good if they are given and bad if they are central. Success is not the standard; it is secondary. As long as whatever we do well, we do for someone or something rather than only ourselves, it is Praise. But if all we're doing is demonstrating our prowess, then we are idolatrous. We become the people of the false God, the false standard. We are in trouble. This much fear taught me.

The meaning to the disabled parts of our selves — to our Sam and Susan — becomes clear once the standards are properly arranged. We are also not to elevate suffering over God. Neither disability nor ability is its own punishment or reward. Even suffering is not primary to a life, even when it is as significant as that which came to Sam or Susan. We are also to do something with our suffering. Jesus used his to save the world. Sam used his to help others. Susan used hers to witness to a proper truth. "I could do nothing else," she tells us. Only care. Only carry on. Only love.

During my burnout, I tried to hide my wounds from my friends and thereby let my suffering go fallow. Actually suffering is fertile. Its use is to break down distance.

Neither ability nor disability, success or failure, accomplishment or shame a track record makes. They are all false standards. When false standards dominate, confusion yields fear. The standard instead is the use to which things are put. The use of ability is praise, to point toward God. The use of suffering is love, to point toward God. Life is relationship, not race, first with God then with each other.

Rather than a track record, Jesus presented wounds. They were able wounds, full of love. They, rather than speed, set the standard for our lives.

Able wounds. Able wounds. The idea rang through my head daily at the end of my first period of apathy. I felt the wounds. I knew I was like those nuns and monks whom Aquinas described as having "acedia." They were prohibited from prayer and praise. Until their sadness of soul ended, they were left alone. I knew I had no joy in my work. I knew my prayers had been reduced to petitions only. I spent too much time worrying about my lost self to really indulge my children.

I descended the mountain into the valley looking for the sources. One was surely the abrupt end of my first marriage and a benighted love affair which followed. Men. The pain underneath the passion of that time was in full bloom. I would not love or be loved in that way again.

I was too old and too committed to other loves. This sadness had the sound of a cell closing, clanking shut, followed only by damp silence. I had depended on romantic love for much of my joy in life; now I was being led to diaper love, daily love, investment love. I had no idea how to do that kind of crockpot love. I had rather liked being a frying pan.

The other source was turning the corner down the mountain. Forty: Not as much time left as has already been. There were some things that I wanted to do that I'd never do. The fear of the irreversible was so much larger than its actuality. I had in fact already lived many lives.

Now I was becoming a person with double normal rather than triple normal energy, and I didn't like it one bit. What exactly did I expect would happen? Fear of loss took over. I didn't know how to renew without a future bigger than the past. I was stuck and couldn't turn the corner.

Not only were the political defeats mounting and the diaper cans overflowing, but my anxiety was the rival of each. I smelled of despair. The church of my youth stunk to high heaven. I was finally the Jacob I had seen in so many others, one wrestling with a dream that had grown too big. The systems all seemed so big and my little groups so small.

It was time to relocate the dream. I wasn't going to live long enough to see the systems overthrown. I was going to have to settle. Settle down, too. It all seemed so dismal. I tried many times to make a David dream to throw at Goliath. But the embarrassment continued. I'd have to eat too many fat words from my happy youth.

Retreat seemed and seems the best strategy. Lick your wounds before making them able. Sit with them. Let them have their say. Clearly that had been a mistake with some of my earlier trouble. I didn't give it the time to become love or forgiveness. I just moved on, shaking the dust off of my feet and my dreams. Some of the dust stuck to my soul.

Some of it didn't go away when I ignored it. It actually grew. Trouble untended is a weed. Once my dreams no longer had a home, a place where they could grow, I became an untended vineyard. Wild. Uncontrollable. Bitchy. Ungrateful. Homeless. A spiritual orphan. Someone who wondered if she had ever had a home. Someone who wandered, even in retreat, desperate for help while trusting absolutely no one to give it.

The fear subsided once I accepted the homelessness as home. Once I realized that this was not the last time I would lay down in a valley and not have the strength to look up, it went away when I wasn't looking.

Once the decision was made to burnout again, to include it as part of my normal life, a lot changed. I became less afraid of over-extension.

I understood that first I would love too much and then I would suffer the consequences. I didn't have to be afraid of my passion and its clear capacity to wound me. Homesickness turned pilgrimage focused my attention forward. The "then" of my former energy was restored to its proper place in an irrepeatable youth. I'd find new levels, maybe even age-appropriate, or I'd be tired. What I wouldn't be was in perpetual mourning.

The best understanding I had of it was as spiritual orphanage, a place where you put things that have unclear origin, and even less clear destination. A place to place the grief that can't be thrown away or weeded out but which no one really wants either.

Did I learn anything from this awful time? Was it all just word games, just replacing "burnout" with "spiritual orphanage"? Or are there some wounds becoming able, ready to move forward with me? Is there anything left to that younger woman who gave this older one birth?

Now I no longer cross off things on my calendar. I check them off. The racing engine is quieter. I don't bounce from one activity to another, I bring their trouble and their test with me. I'm more interested in the meaning of a thing than the doing of it. I go very slow just to make sure I'm seeing everything. I'm scared I'll bypass grief again. Certainly I'll never fall in love again without knowing how much love, while making glad, can also hurt.

Likewise the upward mobility of my false standard has to be enjoyed with all its price tags still attached. Even good things aren't free. There is a cost. I enjoyed success and it crippled me, it made my song come out wrong. I came to be too dependent on its repeating. So dependent that I was sacrificing dreams just to stay "successful."

Like the politics at Seneca, all the messages seem quite mixed up. The good in the bad. The bad in the good. The unevenness of most things. So much of the home I lost was in simplicity. Right and Wrong. Good and Bad. They're all gone now.

Rather than the shrinking of my vital parts, I experienced their expansion, their quickening. *Kolor* was the wilderness; fear was its passage across time. What makes these wounds newly able is what they saw in transit. The capacity to shade. The prediction of future defeat. The knowledge of the orphanage and its many rooms. These aren't anything like the optimisms of my youth. Instead they are my track record, my homesickness turned pilgrimage. Once again I can risk a wound, risk being afraid, risk the pain that will be a life-long partner to passion.

2
dinner at
georgia o'keeffe's
CLASS

dinner at
georgia o'keeffe's
CLASS

You'll PROBABLY BE really impressed if I tell you that once I almost had dinner with Georgia O'Keeffe. That will make you feel closer to one of the greatest modern painters because you'll feel like she is just one of the girls. You'll be glad to know someone who knows someone famous. Or sort of knows someone famous. I never really got to the dinner; I just got invited. I was all ready to go and we were high in the mountains of New Mexico, and Georgia (I'll call her Georgia, just for fun) invited the speakers for that week to her home for dinner. That meant I got to go. And would have gone except that one of the people who had heard my rousing speech on the perils of modern family life for women came to my cabin right at the time I was supposed to leave for dinner at Georgia's, sat down on my bed, and burst into tears. It was about her marriage, her kids, her life. All I could think of was NOW???? Clearly this problem had been going on for a while. Why did it have to erupt just as I was about to get famous? I kept trying to tell her to leave but I couldn't do it. She was sobbing. The marriage truly sounded terrible. I compromised. An hour with her, an hour late to the dinner. By the time I got there, Georgia was sending everyone out the door. She was kind to her neighbors at the conference center but not generous.

The disciples probably felt the same way as I did when Jesus turned down his nose at the chance to sit in the booths with Moses and Elijah. They must have felt that hanging out with the little people kept them from the glories of the bigs. They wanted a little glitter to rub off on them too. But Jesus wasn't that kind of guy. He preferred small places to big systems and probably would have been happy to stay on the bed hearing the broken heart.

Given that I'm a minister and all, I should be glad to be like Jesus. I'm not. I know what the gospel is. I've never been sure I could follow it. I hear it repeat the puzzle that the greatest are the least and the least the greatest. Proportion and scale are the heart of the message. Small is large and large is small; greatest is least and least is greatest. Mountains will be brought down so that valleys can be exalted. I've heard these see-saws from the day I was born, over and over again.

Repetition has made the ears dull. My clear preference for Georgia O'Keeffe over a run-of-the-mill marital problem is the tip of the iceberg. You should see me at cocktail parties; I always gravitate to somebody important and try to impress them.

I'll never forget that on my first summer job I met a family who was living on dandelion greens which they gathered and froze in their freezer. I happened to be working for the Office of Economic Opportunity as what was called an outreach worker. It was my job to find the poor people in Adams County, Pennsylvania, and tell them that the War on Poverty was going on. I spent long twelve-hour days driving around the county going into homes that migrant workers shared with chickens, into barns where a dozen or so children lived with a mother who shot deer in and out of season to feed them. She also shot outreach workers or at least threatened to. But, anyway, it was the Kemp family that really got to me. All those bags and bags of dandelion greens. I couldn't stop thinking about how they ate. Where was their protein? Where were the other vitamins? Finally I got promoted on this job, and it was my job to train other people how to find poor people in the county to go tell them that there was a War on Poverty going on. At first I thought this was terrific. My promotion meant that I could tell other people what to do. I didn't have to talk to poor people anymore at all. I made more money. I was very much more important, and don't think it took me too long to write home to my parents all about it. I told them that yes, in fact, I'd had a promotion on my first job ever, and now I had an office and a desk rather than a clipboard and a front seat. My parents wrote right back with the inevitable question: What are you doing on your new job besides enjoying your new class status? It was pretty embarrassing to have to make up something to tell them, which of course I did, because I didn't want them to be ashamed of me.

The truth of the matter was I was doing nothing. And a lot of it. All day long. I went to a lot of meetings with a lot of other people who weren't doing anything either. We wrote manuals about how to do what we used to do. We had workshops about ways to do what we weren't doing anymore. Every now and then we'd boss around a few of the people who were still driving around the countryside looking for poor people to tell about the War on Poverty. Then it got really weird. Some people who were bigger than even us started coming in and asking a lot of questions, demanding that we produce some real live poor people at some of our meetings.

We'd actually beg poor people to come to those meetings. If it hadn't been for Mr. and Mrs. Kemp, who seemed to be awfully healthy for just eating dandelion greens, if it hadn't been for them actually getting some real live poor people to come to our meetings when our big bosses would come to town, I'd have probably lost that job where I did nothing and got paid well for it.

I guess these were the times when I got all hot and bothered about "bureaucracy," a big word to describe what happened to the War on Poverty but a good one nonetheless. Bureaucracy was the traitor in that war, it was the spy. What happened was that big and little got reversed; like in a Greek tragedy, they were out of whack. Imagine what would have happened if all that money had stuck with the little people instead of detouring to the bigs. I was too well-trained in the art of moving up not to climb. I wanted to see Georgia O'Keeffe and so we just went off to see her, leaving behind the people who had called us there in the first place.

It would be one thing if twenty years ago in the War on Poverty, by chance, this tragedy happened, and from then on big systems like bureaucracy had kept small places like Adams County, Pennsylvania, out of trouble. But that's not how it's been going. Twenty years later I moved to a small town on the eastern end of Long Island. I moved there because of the well-integrated, high quality, small public school in the town.

I visit the school before coming; I marvel at the teachers, I anticipate with glee how much my three small children are going to like this school. I delight in their going to a small school in a small place that hasn't forgotten yet who or what it is. I tell everyone I know that the teachers actually like the school, that they like teaching there. I tell them how centrally located the school is, next to the train station, close to the main street and the churches and the library. I wax. I want something little to be central. Lo and behold, I get to Riverhead and the school board has recommended closing the school. Consolidating it. Making it larger and regional.

Big systems chase small places. They have chased me all over the country and, with my active participation, ruined more than one home to which I have fled for refuge.

Before we get the good guys and the bad guys mixed up, let's be as clear as possible that I like a big system as well as anybody. Remember whom I gravitate to at cocktail parties. I'm still mad about missing Georgia O'Keeffe's roast duckling. My climbing boots are as weathered as anyone's; upward mobility is my Everest. I love it when I discover that I not only painted my kitchen an unusual color but that *Good Housekeeping* thinks it's a Santa Fe color.

I may be hopeless but I know that I want something better and smaller for my children. I've learned something climbing. I've learned what's wrong with big. How much harm big does is what's wrong with big. The main thing that's wrong with schools is that they're too big. They do harm when they get too big. They harm teachers, and principals, and custodians, and then they go on to harm children. The teachers feel out of control; the kids feel like numbers. I want them to avoid as long as possible feeling like a number. To lose a small, good school and make it into a larger, bigger school, to throw away decades of a tradition of excellence, and goodness, and integration at the heart of a small town is crazy. You'd only do it because you forgot that the mountains are becoming valleys and the valleys, mountains. You'd only do it because you wanted the bigs to have more power than the littles. What has happened in our land is that big has gotten too big for its britches. Hospitals are really too big to do healing, and prisons are too big to handle repentance, and schools are too big to permit education. In each of those big systems something larger than the avowed purpose is going on. What's going on is bureaucracy, that system of accountability which has made big systems too big and small places too small to allow good things to happen.

These things happen in the church as well, don't worry. Many pastors have decided that calling is too small an activity for them to do, so they work like crazy to hire an associate so they have somebody to be bigger than. If not an associate, then a retired calling pastor, or at least a Sunday School person; or if not that, a student. Even pastors forget what a glory it is to have a job where you get to do everything, including taking out the garbage and delivering the flowers. In some crazy place in our heads, we want to be bigger. The higher we are on the ladder of bureaucracy, the bigger we feel.

Eventually we have to count the costs. The loss of Mr. and Mrs. Kemp as friends was a high price for me to pay. Many parents learn that pushing their kids to upward mobility means pushing them right out of town. It means pictures, not laps full of grandchildren. As businesses grow, they learn that it's no longer cost effective to employ older people, no matter the years of relationship in the fraternity of the morning coffee truck. We also learn what our kids learn: they figure out soon enough that because they are small they must be unimportant.

Class is something Americans don't think they have. The cost in that deception alone is monumental. By disallowing class and climbing as explanations for our misery, we are barred from getting to the bottom of it. It's like having a virus and deciding that you don't have it and looking at every other diagnosis too intently from then on. A lot of American misery comes from class being out of whack; it comes from climbing.

Like most Americans I figure if I'm unhappy it must be my fault. Insufficient effort or negative mental attitude are my demons. The work ethicists grab me on the way in and the psychologists pound me on the way out. Coming or going I take the rap. It is therefore no accident that I blame poverty on the poor. If I see my own situation as a function of the self, then why would I treat them any better than I treat me?

My youth had the excellence of a small town nestled in one of the many armpits of the great Hudson River. In the 1950's the river not only smelled; it smelled unrepentantly. Environmentalists had yet to have their say or way with it, and so when we went swimming at the point, we simply swam around the oil pools and other industrial effluents. Little did we know at eight, nine, or ten that the day would come when we couldn't swim away from these effluents, that slowly they would circle us and make us feel like the unwanted body in the river.

Excellent it was, though, because neither the child in me nor the immaturity of a post-war nation appreciated yet what was coming. Like the ice skaters at Dinky's Pond, we could still glide over the surface of back-breaking change. Even the armpits couldn't hold their peace against it eventually; the peace was phony, the armpit antagonized.

Then, I knew plenty of poor people and thought they were normal. I was poor only on my father's side so already I was getting a disquieting feeling of more than one world. My mother's family had these awful expectations: they planned on improving just about everything and everybody. On my father's side, the Naccarattos, with their seven children and beer bellies, planned on nothing improving and thus woke up the neighborhood morning and night with the bird call of family disharmony.

That I was prohibited from playing with Charlie made this the more interesting. He was the first fast-talking juvenile delinquent of my acquaintance, and I owe a great deal of the success of my ministry to his short course in con artistry. His mother worked. Everyone said that and drug out the word "worked" until it snaked into a sneer. Once I found Charlie crying in a big hole in the ground where we used to play hide and sneak between the weeds. He never did say what was wrong. At Dinkys' he skated too fast when they would let him in. He knew the tributaries to the pond as well as the main circles and kept them clear of snow. Some girls skated up there with him but not me. I had higher expectations. That's not true. I was frequently scared of adventure.

Shirley and Sharon and Judy were my friends on the lower side of Kingston near the dirty river, across the tracks. Not until the women's movement of the 1970s did I again have such close female friends. I competed unmercifully with the upper-class girls like Judy. I was to meet many girls with larger charge accounts than Judy's mother but never to dislike another quite as much as Judy's. She had a way of making my father's side so unwelcome that I think my hems did fall out when I went into her house. The number of times she indicated that Judy couldn't play with me now because Judy had to practice the piano should have placed Judy with Liberace. No such luck. Judy died on the New York State Thruway at nineteen, coming home from college in a snowstorm, all her music lessons and expectations with her.

My friends had a way of dying young. Not just the river or Kingston but real friends died. Personal ones. I was pitcher on a state championship softball team and Sue was the catcher. One day she had a brain tumor and the next day she was gone. Another friend, Frank, shut himself up in a garage and melted his brain. He is known as alive but that's all. Oddly each of these tragedies took less of a toll than the river. There was something normal about death, even youthful death. Something accidental and small.

The pollution of the river was done on purpose. It started and stopped with human decision. It didn't have to be, whereas Frank's despair was almost necessary. When people can't love and don't love over a long period of time, they create consequences. Frank was a consequence.

You couldn't blame these deaths on class, on climbing and getting a boot in your face. I tried to do that with Frank, to argue that his mother's house was too small, that her clothes were too worn, and his also, and thus the despair. Sue had the same background but her tumor came by chance; Frank did it to himself. I was often so desperate for an explanation with Frank that I'd use anything. He talked me out of class, thus allowing me to diagnose it more appropriately. I figured out that it wasn't a blanket, just a large throw. Class explained only some, not all, things.

One time about a year before he did it, he came to a little farm we had in Pennsylvania. It was fall and yellow, and we walked the full day of color. That time and that talk was so good that it almost challenges the terror of the wintry day his full-size special bus pulled up in front of my Chicago door and let off what was left of the person I knew as Frank. His various parts were simply no longer well connected. Nor could he talk. If I listened very carefully I could hear his voice. "Forgiven" was the word he was saying.

Anyway, there has been death and loss, and my small systems help me bear the personal parts; and the big systems — they aren't mine, so how could I call them that — the big systems harm even my capacity to heal. They do that by misdirecting my attention away from friends and community toward climbing. If there weren't other friends left when some of my friends died, I don't know what I'd do. Fortunately very few people have stranded me in cabins of tears and gone off to have dinner with Georgia O'Keeffe.

At least when I'm wasting my time climbing, I can remember the health of small places. I know what music will sound like in Charlie's living room. I know how the Kemps would see Georgia O'Keeffe's paintings, politely and passionlessly. They would not see themselves as people who paintings are for. They might even see paintings as against them.

The whole business of class transcends place. It's everywhere, investing every age with its separations and its discriminations. I am tempted to be glad I got my leg up, that I don't have to be where my father's family started. I don't have to eat their food, or enjoy their velvet paintings, or drink their beer, or tell their jokes, or fight their bosses, or watch their TV all night.

I don't even have to improve things the way my mother's people do. Their fear that their clothes aren't quite right is a respectability my education has forsaken. I don't even have to mourn the river anymore. Worse things have happened: a Christmas bombing at Bach Mai is a much more upscale sadness. King is dead. You know the possibilities for grief. There are plenty of injuries. I could even let the Hudson go.

All these places I don't have to be! No wonder every time I hear a news broadcast about the homeless I assume they're talking about me. A resident of the world, a boarder at civilization's boarding house, a roamer, a vagabond. In better moods I'd say pilgrim or sojourner and dress up all this sadness with an Easter bonnet. But not today. Not most days. It takes a few drinks, or a few friends, or the right light to evoke the happiness all this sadness has made possible.

Unlike Frank, whom no one wanted, everyone wanted me. Up and down the ladder. My father and his world have been nothing but insulted since the day I left for college. "Too big for her britches," they would say.

My mother and her world make constant invitations to return. "Act normal," says their imperialism. "Where do you get off thinking you're any different or better than us? You don't follow the rules. You dress weird. You don't have the money to back up the freedom you claim. Be careful." And on it goes, class for class, until we all wake up knowing just the decibel and degree to which our rung on the ladder permits us. Income, $42,000; house, $140,000; children, piano but not skiing lessons; tracking well in their dog run at school; vacation, Aruba not St. Thomas, etc. Markets have analyzed us better than we ourselves. And yet the fictions persist about a classless society; the movies flatter the little people and we all cry.

My parents started all this demand for shelter. They moved away from Kingston when I was eleven, and they never stopped moving and neither did I. We moved so much that only the road was home. Their roots were so bruised by the move away from the only home they had known that they never again walked without a limp. I've spent more time in my life trying to figure out why they left their home on the river than I've spent on anything else.

I return and return to that decision like a moth to a flame. As we pulled off Second Avenue, the Red Ball van packed with all that was left of my childhood, my mother cried and cried. She'd wanted to be braver. Maybe we three kids cried too; I don't know. It is her tears that I remember.

She was crying for the river, but I don't think she knew it. More fairly put, I think she was crying over the river; she thinks she was mourning her mother, and a few friends, and a bakery with good jelly doughnuts and crumb cakes, German butchers, and her high school. I claim the big system in her tears and she the small places, and we have fought over this concentric circle for two solid decades, ever since I realized why factories closed up north and moved south.

She argues that our decision to leave Kingston was an act of personal, intentional freedom. We moved there so my father could get a better job and we could go to college. Upward mobility I suppose you'd call it, if by upward mobility you mean children having to practice Southern accents in front of mirrors so other children wouldn't make fun of their Yankee tones. Or you could mean that it is a participation in some pain for the sake of larger pleasures. Like walking in a new classroom in the fall so you'd know Shakespeare later, or not having your father home six months at a time so that you'd know to soften brie before serving it.

She sees freedom in these motions, like trading up to first class for your next airplane trip to Omaha. I feel more like I just rented a car, asked for the compact because it would get me to all the places I wanted to go, and they handed me a Lincoln Continental because that's all that was available. I should be happy, you see, and I'm not.

I really don't know what I feel. I'd have to know how it would have been staying in Kingston, with the garment industry gone, IBM coming and going, scaring all the workers all the time, substituting sandwiches in Saran Wrap off the truck, old and stale, for the oily ones made with Sal's dirty hands and lots of onion. The juice just dried up in Kingston.

Learning a new accent in front of a mirror is better than repeating the same old dirty words to sophomores at Kingston High School. I had already read everything in that dinky library and they closed the ice pond down. The town sponsors recreation now.

The fact that we moved not just once but three times after leaving Kingston meant that we got to repeat the moving van scene over and over. My father would leave in December and take the new job. We'd follow after school let out. If it weren't for church youth groups to act as a sanctuary for my homelessness, I'd never have made it out of adolescence alive. The terror of a new school in the seventh, ninth, and tenth grades still makes me shy in an aggressive sort of way. I'd repeat over and over to myself, ''They're just as scared of something else as I am of walking into these rooms.''

Projecting the fear allowed me to move up, as I was scripted, as a whole generation of movers were condemned to do.

People kept swimming back in the Hudson but we never understood how. In the south the water was clean of abandoned factories. Imagine how weird it is to prefer dirty water. It wasn't really the dirt; it was the history, mine and the region's all gone, all visible by a deep staring through the oil slick. Not gone seminaturally, like Frank or Susan; gone by choice, like a successful suicide.

Killed. Too many unions in the North. Let's fly. Too many uppity blacks. Let's flee. Too much family. Mother-in-laws butting in over everything from what the kids had for dinner to what they wore to Sunday School. Aunts and uncles everywhere with half of them needing money and the other half needing a muzzle. The house was loud with relatives. The phone rang with my mother's friends all the time. Then it got so quiet and so clean. I couldn't bear her loneliness anymore, especially when she would say she liked it.

She never understood how desperate I was for a mother when my children were born. I wanted someone to buttinski with information about their food and no one did. I had hurt having the holidays every year with no one as a kid; I hurt having the holidays with another group of well-educated friends as an adult. She couldn't admit the loneliness, and I couldn't stop talking about it.

We are practically an emotional cross. I am surrounded by friends, my Christmas card list is too long, and I love time alone. She is the reverse. And a playwright could go on for three acts showing how we've passed our sorrow back and forth across the generations. High school students could diagram the emotional flow. She would be sure I was nuts even thinking about this. It would be like that time I asked her to read the book about mothers and daughters, and she read it, only to suggest that I take a long vacation. These are the consequences of upward mobility: crossed generations, homelessness, suffering that some can name and others can't.

She floated over the big system of industrial flight that determined her life, and I went to war against it. Probably the venom with which I fight that war is a gift to her. She would prefer more dependable Mother's Day greetings. Since she doesn't want or need the gift, I give it to the Hudson. It I can still romanticize.

It becomes the big system flowing through the small places. It connects without dehumanizing. Of course it's dirty and polluted because it's more like history than anything else.

Of course my mother has freedom under the new arrangement. In South Carolina, there are buffets everywhere, dozens of sodas, multiple cinemas, pretty beaches. There is abundant leisure and even tradition. But it will never be for my family; we are stuck with the leisure untethered to any tradition.

We moved there freely. No one made us. We played the upward mobility chip and we won the hand. Winning the game is more complicated. Then you have to count what you lost as well as what you won. We lost most of what we started the game with: family, tradition, and place. New rivers flow in our new towns but not one of our long-gone children swam in them.

All the stories of Judy and Sharon and Shirley come by telephone, with the tin unique to speaker phones. They are also long distance, brief, curtailed, measurable by the phone company. We lost good stories when we lost traditional space.

Odd, isn't it, that knowing so much of the grief of big system upward mobility I should still prefer Georgia O'Keeffe? Just because we know what hurt our parents doesn't mean we won't invite it to hurt us as well.

Our parents encourage us with these denials. Maybe we are missing something. Everybody else wants to move up, why shouldn't we? Maybe some schools actually improve when con-solidated. Maybe there is a good bureaucracy somewhere. Just because the one you worked in almost made you forget what you knew about the poor, their normalcy; just because bureaucracy tried to teach you to treat the poor as clients, that doesn't mean all bureaucracies are stupid. If they were, surely your parents would have fought them more than they did.

You see why you need the river. You need it to get back home. To try to remember what you knew. But when you get back home you may find out that the truth you knew was divided. Forked.

Cross-currented. That your parents believed they are responsible for their middle-classness, like the poor are responsible for their poverty. And you know that's not true or only a little bit so. And then you need the river to get away. Dinky's has to be escaped right after it's recovered. It was dinky to your parents too.

But the river won't stop to assign responsibility. It will carry the very pollution that is destroying it on its back, its moving van. It will ferry those who move away from home as well as those forced away from home. It takes no sides. Can it bring you back? Only romantics think so.

Forward is the more important question. So now, with the river's neutrality, parental freedom, dirty water, and dirty linen all aired, we begin to forget what we have to and remember what we need.

The poor are no more responsible for their poverty than the rich for their wealth or the middle for their middle. We are responsible for how we understand these things, not for what they are. What they are is industries chasing markets and labor. What they are include geopolitics and racial flight; what they are include the best hopes parents have for their children and their worst fears. What they are is neither all good or bad, rather it is a mixture, a serious bank along a serious river where individual choice is real but limited.

If we begin to understand the isness of place or class, the genuine otherness of systems that determine our place and class, rather than assuming personal responsibility, just imagine. My mother and I might be able to get along. Rich and poor, needy and capable, despairing and hopeful might imagine a right to places at the table. As it is now even the government thinks the poor have rights to services, not places. They need workers to work on them. Is it any wonder that I prefer O'Keeffe's capacity to a stranger's need? Frank thinks having no hope means he has no place.

Each belongs, but few know it or want it. My family, unlike me, deeply belonged in their place. But they let it go and thus condemned me to a search for "belonging" I'm not sure I deserve. You see how the system's morality works? Toxic wastes I assume I deserve. A good place I figure I have to work for.

Upstream on the river, that place forward, where nobody I know lives, yet. Up there, these matters will be different. Both good and bad will be matters of grace. Only place will be deserved.

3
when the
skylights went in

AGING

when the
skylights went in

AGING

As JUST ABOUT everyone knows, with the clear exception of my three children, there are some things you don't do in church. You don't travel under the pews. You don't laugh during the hymns. You don't pong your brother. You don't wave at your friends or insist on Tic-Tac mints as a bribe to sit through the longer lessons. In church one behaves with respect. One dresses appropriately. Appropriate even extends too often to keeping quiet when you don't like what is going on. You are not to interrupt the minister even if she bores you. Inappropriate covers a lot of sins.

Some things are equally appropriate. Eating another piece of good cake at a friend's house may be good for her ego and bad for your body. Thus it's both right and wrong not to. You can also be appropriate in different ways. Like the time I left home in Martinsburg, West Virginia, to go off to college, wearing a seersucker suit and stockings and short-heeled pumps, only to arrive at a college on the first day where everyone else was wearing T-shirts. My clothes were appropriate to the college I saw across the hills in West Virginia but not appropriate to the one that existed close up in Pennsylvania. Since this problem with the gray seersucker suit, I've decided that the truly inappropriate were those who decided to dress down for the occasion and that the day would come soon enough when they'd have enough deprivation to appreciate education enough to get dressed for it.

Jesus knew all these things. He was neither culturally illiterate or unmannered. He knew that merchants had been in the temple for centuries, that they were there so people could travel long distances for Passover without the burden of a sacrificial lamb. They could change their money to the Tyrian shekel when they arrived and buy their lamb there. Early take-out sort of the idea.... The money changers were thus as legitimate as 7-Eleven.

So why did he throw them out? Why did he violate what was

appropriate to do something he thought more appropriate? Why, when confronted with two appropriates, did he choose anger over polite repression? Worse, did he make a mistake liking the temple better than Bingo, or was he acting like he was too good to make a buck? What galled him so that his own gentleness took a back seat to his own anger?

Maybe this is the reason. Maybe he loved the temple too much. If you love the gospel, you have to interrupt a minister who is boring you with it. If you love the gospel, sometimes you have to get angry. You have to be mad when what you love is hurt. If you don't throw the merchants out of the temple, then you become their victim, their victory. Jesus knew too well the difference between love and indifference. He had no choice but to be angry at the temple when it violated itself. Scholars are quite convinced that this anger cost him his life. The Sadducees and Pharisees can't tolerate inappropriate behavior.

Inappropriate behavior creates chaos, it shifts power, it heats things up, and gives too many too much to talk about. Like love, it brings in from the cold out of doors that feeling of being out of control. No doubt there's a little bit of Pharisee in all of us. We had hoped to become more in control of things as we got older, and look what happens. As love takes root in us, we find ourselves losing control.

Fear of losing control is at the root of much of the indifference that has seeded my soul. In a truly proper temple, however, anger would be no stranger. Love would require its presence. Temples do violate themselves. Things get out of control. No one lives too long without learning this fact. My hunch is that the same merchants who brought in the animals for Passover sacrifice probably charged a fair price in the beginning, just like lovers tolerate more messy toothpaste tubes in the earlier years of a relationship, and new bakeries bake better bread, and writers who are lean and hungry write better poetry, and builders build better houses when they're starting out. When I was a teenager, I thought love was freedom itself: Now I know it is a beautiful bondage. We do cut corners, and the more indifferent we become to our task or temple, the more corners we cut. The less we expect. The more we tolerate. The more we become afraid of the very anger which is required to restore the temple or the task. Anger purifies. No wonder so many of us are so dirty. Isn't it odd that we think being dirty is being appropriate?

Life is at least these choices: to be out of control by being indifferent or out of control by loving. If indifferent, you give the temple over to the merchants who violate it. You don't have to worry about anger for long because pretty soon you become incapable of it. When love leaves so does the capacity for anger. If love stays, however, you get to be out of control because neither anger nor love comes with a warranty. Throwing the merchants out the front door, no matter how angrily or lovingly, doesn't mean they won't come back in the back door tomorrow. Ask any addict: we know. Plus, with love and anger, there's always the chance somebody with more power to enforce the appropriates will decide that you're not that and join the Pharisees in trying to get rid of you.

Jesus did not see these two choices of how to be out of control as equally appropriate. He saw the proper temple as the place where love belonged and indifference did not. The Pharisees and Sadducees did not see it that way. And here's the reason Jesus did not live a long or normal life. Simply put, he thought indifference was inappropriate.

It's easy to understand that love is appropriate. All signs point in that direction. But few of us age appropriately. I forgive just about everybody sixty for not coming out to night meetings. I understand what people mean when they talk about the old ladies in the congregation. People mean that they have little energy, little money, lots of time, but no capacity to spend it on developing the institution. People almost never talk kindly about the old ladies. Worse, the old ladies don't even talk nicely about themselves: they talk nicely about who they used to be, and what they used to stand for, but current speech revolves around what is gone and lost.

In my youth I feared that the old were hopelessly indifferent. They shared less and less about more and more. This wasn't so much a matter of night meetings as a matter of style. Cé la vie. Cum si, cum sa. I got the impression that it was too much effort to care.

Now as I hear the local American Association of Retired Persons staff member advise the "Seniors" to vote against anything with the word school in it, I bristle against the self-directedness of their caring. I see selfishness, not indifference. Retaining the capacity to care about something besides yourself strikes me as one of the real challenges. Keeping indifference off must be a lot like keeping pounds off; it requires that something matter more than the easy bite or the recliner chair.

I wish I saw more examples of age-appropriate behavior. For that matter, I'd enjoy less indifference among the young. But the correlation of age and indifference is so complete that we almost give the long-lived permission not to care. Almost as though we expect them — and therefore ourselves — to care less while aging, as though these things were automatic.

I certainly used to care more about my house's appearance, or my own, than I do now. I sense both that fewer people are looking and that I don't really care too much about what those few think when they do look. Living with myself has become much more important than the respect of others. Jaded seems to me to be a certainty. I care less what others think because I have less respect for them or how they think. People have turned out to be less than I thought they were going to be. I think this downward curve in the opinion polls that the race takes over time is almost universal. I have yet to meet a person for whom the direction is upward.

On that basis alone how dare I expect some elderly to care more over time? Why is indifference so hard to swallow? Just because Jesus thought it inappropriate, so what? Are not the old wise? Is indifference not age-appropriate?

If the answer comes "yes" to these questions, no doubt a review of the enthusiasms of youth is not far behind. Do they qualify as love or simply another expression of the self's energy and biology?

These questions are too big. They invoke the general as guide to the particular, and there's no warrant for it. Wherever big systems invade small places, the danger is oppression. As individuals we may choose to age indifferently or, as I suspect, to simply care more selectively. What is obnoxious is predictions of these passages. They make the child in me want to revolt, to care longer than anyone else has just for the oppositeness of it.

But I can't care much more than I already do. The limits on my energy are severe. I've gone from having the energy of three average people to having the energy of two. The disappointment, the loss, is wreaking havoc with all I know of size and scale. I am embarrassing myself frequently.

This kind of energy gets quickly overdone. It doesn't know how to stop. Thus I indulge the question of appropriate, of how much caring is right for me. Would I ever feel satisfied at any level? I think not. The energy of five people would no doubt bother me as much as the energy of two. We Americans despise limits; it comes with the territory.

When I have chanced into limits, I've had good experience. For example, I never could figure how many calls would be appropriate for a parish. I felt I was never calling enough. Finally I divided the membership by forty-eight working weeks in a year and decided that number was the appropriate number of visits per week. Tithing achieves the same peace. Maybe someday I'll know how many letters per year a good friend should get or how many special moments a son or daughter needs in a day. Or the right order for stern exercise and soft relaxation. Or the proper number of times children should have some homemade cookies per year. Until these figures arrive, I predict the growth of indifference at the sheer number of appropriate questions.

Answers to these questions are crucial to maturity. Otherwise one stands permanently accused by the amount of care the world needs. To care with the energy one has — even if it decreases eventually to zero — is very different from indifference. When truly old, if truly unable to care, can the heart turn, the mind remember, the soul stare? More questions that need to go on a diet.

The leaves were gone when the skylights went in. Age came sooner than the ability to spot it.

I never thought I'd be old or forty. Not that anyone else did either, but the lack of foresight deserves mention anyway. It's the problem with aging more than aging itself. We boomers have ridden a demographic wave that always reflected us back to ourselves at twice the size. Born after a war and depression that oddly threw our limitless nation into prominence, we skated through our childhoods sure of our place in history. Churches built new Sunday Schools for us, schools consolidated, and advertisers made it their business to predict our next whim. We have been way too televised for our own good. Our parents insisted we better them and hated us when we did. It was an odd time to try to grow up. The feeling was of always being in the first act with the curtain going up and up, until it made you dizzy just watching it.

Now as the aches and pains arrive, barely the match for the chicken pox of our postponed children, we realize that it's too late to grow up. If we haven't done so by now, we may not ever.

It's actually going to be quite difficult to blame aging on a big system. Apparently people aged before the industrial revolution and will do so afterward. The romantic poets didn't have superhighways to accuse for their balding: They accused nakedly, without excuses, raging against the dying of the night, wanting death to mother beauty and all that excessive hope, long before the advent of anti-wrinkle cream.

Hard as it will be to blame the big system for the cellulite on our thighs, we system-bashers will surely try. We'll blame the lack of preparation on our environment, the way the Junior League blames the custodian for an improper set-up of the tables for the luncheon, petulantly, with a full petticoat of privilege implied.

It's true that we are not prepared. They put cemeteries in the middle of towns, all the graves snuggled together. You go there only to bury the dead or walk the dog. If these emblems of death could be scattered about, maybe we wouldn't be so surprised. Next to the hardware store, where you go to fix what is broken, it would be nice to see a slate reminding us that not everything will repair. The hospitals hide the sick from us equally efficiently, and now the nursing homes keep the toothless away, probably out of concern that they might scare us. What really scares us is that we've forgotten how close we, and not just they, are to the other side. We've had too few reminders.

My own trip to these so-called morbidities is about as dull as anyone's. Until recently I had one of those bodies that loved abuse. Stay up all night as often as possible was its creed, forgetting meals its motto, hyperactivity its liturgy. Add in my enjoyment of tobacco and liquor, and you have a good picture of the star athlete "growing up." Then came thirty-nine. The birth of twins at thirty-eight left me with a hiatus hernia that required frequent small meals as tribute. All of a sudden one day I realized that I couldn't see the newspapers, and the doctor confirmed serious loss of sight. "But," told I him, "I've always had 20-20 vision." "But," he told me, "now you're forty, and your eyes are wearing out." He actually then laughed. He was all of thirty-two, still capable of aging jokes. The day before yet another young doctor had told me that the pain in my foot was not just pain: it was arthritis. You can imagine how bored stiff I am by all of this.

Like I said, the skylights went in long after the leaves were gone. I was less than ready to look out the window that aging provided. But there it was, the opening, the clear blue sky that confirmed all the wisdom I'd heard only to use on other people while abstaining myself. I was immortal; "they" had reason to appreciate "limits," to see the more in less, the quality over the quantity. From my new bedroom windows, with the new skylights November installed, I saw stone clear winter blue, trees firmly outlined, leaves all gone, excess stripped away by necessity not choice, shape and contour all. I was getting wintry. I was growing old.

The first clue I followed was in the word *age-appropriate*. Would I have to toss half my wardrobe? Was my hair right for a middle-aged person? I knew therapists used *age-appropriate* as a way to tell how sick you were. I used it once when a very mature and overly responsible twenty-two year old gave me a heavy metal album to listen to. Finally, I told him, you've done something age-appropriate. But that clue dissolved when I realized that age-appropriate was more and more indifference, more curving in on my self and my prescriptions and proscriptions. The avoidance of death was becoming a matter of too much importance. Time for living was being lost.

There are a lot of us today who are trying to throw the merchants out of the temples of our bodies. We are trying to purify our health. We don't cook with salt, or eat real butter, or smoke cigarettes, or fry bacon. We ride bicycles in our living rooms: we walk and talk endlessly about it. We all know our cholesterol levels and our blood pressures. Fiber is actually a subject of extensive discussion, and if you get my mother-in-law going on salt, you'll never get out of her kitchen. What she feels about hardened arteries most people reserve for the Nazis.

I got in an elevator the other day with a man at just about noon. I was on my way to something lite [*sic*], and he had in his hand two cigars and a candy bar. I guess I stared a second too long because he said to me apologetically, ''Usually I have a yogurt, but today I'm in a lousy mood.'' I mumbled my own apology because I really wasn't thinking anything about what he was having for lunch. It was like I had caught him in the act. Smoking gun in the hand. Merchants in the temple. He was not doing his part for everlasting life. In fact, if he kept up those lunches, he'd be lucky to make it to sixty. Some of us would want him out of our insurance group.

Those of us who are carrying a little more belly than we should, or supporting more of a defense budget than we should, tune in right here. We could be ideal weight or ideal morally, but we're not. Jesus' promise of everlasting life is seductive when it's not being a total pain. Enormous possibility — even for health or peace — is obnoxious. Oddly, reflections on death invite reflections on perfection, on everlasting, on where all the goodness was or is. While living, we become very acquainted with imperfection, that's the reason.

At mid-life I lost the clue about appropriate that I was following, and I started following the clue about perfection. Thus I started to think about the words *everlasting life* and what they meant. I really wanted to poke fun at us health buffs. We seemed to be after everlasting life as the result of our own efforts and also to be punitive against those who did not practice good habits. At first it seemed important to clarify everlasting life as a gift and not a get because of the danger and cruelty of being well by reason of one's own virtue. What do you say to those who have rheumatoid arthritis? Have they done something wrong? This is an old Christian problem. Blaming blindness in the child on the sin of the father. Blaming mental illness on adultery. Blame, blame, blame as though sin explained everything. Jesus fought that assignment of blame. Invoking possibilities, not punishments, was his method.

But still I wanted to expose the health movement and its abundant theologic inaccuracies. You can really have a lot of fun with peanut butter as salvation. But the more I thought about the promise of eternal life, the more possible it became, the more worthy of effort it seemed. More jogging and purer peanut butter were less the point. They were simply actions reflecting possibility as opposed to efforts toward it. They respond to the merchants in the temple by throwing them out and in so doing are acts of bodily love rather than indifference. Cigars and candy bars are bodily indifferent. I've concluded that there's nothing wrong with the wellness movement that a little humor can't fix.

Everlasting is bodily and then some. We find our images for it in each other. In the fearlessness of those who die among us; in the fearlessness of the many who have already died and who live in us and through us by what they taught or showed or gave; or in the sense that when bodies are defeated, spirits still thrive; or in the fears that we give to each other when our bodies are hurting; in all these ways, we come to some things that last. They turn out to be glimpses of perfection, or at least everlasting possibility. Ever is probably too big a word. I personally don't need everlasting as much as I need lasting. I do need to be surrounded by some things that I'll never forget. Spirits that refuse fear some of the time, healthy attitudes toward pain and suffering, the myriad ways ordinary people have of sleeping nights while waiting till Thursday for the test results, the ways others have of being aware of more than the persistent leg cramp or removed breast, these things last long enough for me to listen to what Jesus is saying about everlasting. Such possibilities become easier to entertain not so much as I watch my diet and habits — which I do as long as they don't get in the way of my living — but rather they become easier to entertain because of all the ordinary courage that is around.

Everlasting seems to be a hope on which a lot that is lasting can be found.

Mostly as I thought about aging, I tried to rearrange my thoughts. They were like a closet that hadn't been cleaned out since high school. I wanted to age appropriately but hadn't the slightest idea how to. I wanted to flirt with the future, even the possibility of everlasting as a future, but ended up settling for a permanent anti-merchant posture with heavy leanings to possibilities. I also made some plans. I did not just tackle the mental closet.

When we first hatched the idea of the Susan B. Anthony Nursing Home, we were just kidding. We had eggs to spare. Now we're dead serious and almost late for our last appointment, the same way we've been for so many before. I was late to civil rights, late to Vietnam, had my abortion late, and smoked marijuana late. My cohorts in the nursing home idea were always more on time: they had a way of introducing me to the future, of always acting like it was normal to go places you'd never been before. They tried to prepare me for later earlier.

We have to find a place with a big porch and a pretty view. It has to be geographically congenial with room for all of our individualism to coexist with our collectivity. The nurses don't have to be hired yet; we have to disagree on details for a least a decade. Echoes of the old fight about men will have to reverberate, and some decision about whether they're allowed will have to emerge. Lesbian and straight women need more time to distrust each other before we coalesce our pension checks. What happened before will happen again, the see-saw of fights and reconciliations. Surely these things take time to run their course. We'll all be a little different. Who knows if youthful exuberance will be around to carry us through the next generation of quarrels? Who knows if we'll land in our rocking chairs friends or enemies?

What I've decided is that our personal temperatures probably don't matter. We're good enough friends for warm and cold to mix it up with each other. And I'd rather risk my future on friendship than bureaucracy. The way I see it we're condemned to each other, like husband and wife and mother and daughter. Our choices are to let the state or private enterprise take "care" of us or to take care of ourselves. The only way to avoid tottering down Broadway on the arm of our private nurse is to create the capacity to share the nurse. We don't have to like each other for that. If friendship can survive entrepreneurial socialism, all the better. No one else has lived the history of our market segment. Ha. We are the sixties turned feminist, turned superwomen, turned mothers, turned women ministers, turned old. We are a peculiar blot on the screen. If we don't go into business for our own retirements, who will? Strangers? Governments? Profiteers? Most of the religious nursing homes to which we would ordinarily go probably pray to God "the Father," morning, noon, and night. That threat alone should foster cooperation. Such prayers would cause even higher blood pressure than our environments have already produced.

Necessity being the mother of invention and all that, it's past time to draw up the disagreements. Part-time utopians that we are, living the front end of our lives integrated, won't we have fun enacting the threat we've made so often to separate? So often we've judged ourselves weird enough to require time away, out of normal society, in a place safe enough that we wouldn't have to explain everything. We've threatened to leave, quit, run away, make our own separate world.

You never know when it's too late to act on that threat. Or too early. To walk out on the inhumanity of it all is to walk out on the humanity as well. We may be too blended to separate. Or we may realize our larger fear: that we were always too separate to blend. Vacillating between separation and society has become our way of life. First to the institutional church's meeting where we load ourselves down with work, then to the outsider's meeting where we load our quivers, then to the support group that holds our flung-apartness together, then home, then work, then collapse, then standing on two feet again, always late, always more places to go than time to get there.

I think at retirement one has to jump off this merry-go-round. I think finally the energy runs out. The flung-apartness no longer holds. Or maybe you just keep being late for appointments.

The leaves were long gone when the skylights went in, so I'll admit I didn't know about the choices until it was almost too late. I didn't see enough of what was going on. Couldn't see the forest for the trees. There was this recurring sense that I could decide all that morality stuff later, that the expediency of making sure everyone liked me would carry me until I was old enough to determine a moral course. I allowed the merchants free reign of the temples, never realizing how at home they had become.

My first marriage ended because I couldn't figure out how to say what hurt me. I compromised my own position by silence. One terrible job I had, which carried the responsibility of a generation of urban ministers, I blew in a big way, for lots of reasons beyond my own control, but nevertheless including the fact that I couldn't face evil. I kept trusting the compromisers. I kept thinking they would eventually remember the mission of the church, that now they were just too busy, but later they'd see the fading light. They never did. I trusted way too long. If I could have blown the whistle earlier, if I could have made fewer excuses for them, I would be able to be less ashamed of how, rather than carrying my friend's water, I spilled it.

Not alone but together, I let nuclear power and bombs get way too close to my children and community. This capacity I have to tolerate the merchants in the temple is large. I found out by my failures that it was too late, not too early, to throw them out, to make choices about whose walk you want to be on and to make them clearly. Sluffing those choices has caused me most of the pain in my life, while making them has produced most of the joy. The big system of youthful pragmatism poisoned too many of my small places, including my body, which I obviously thought was ageless.

There remain huge pockets of appropriate indifference, and I suspect I will take them to the grave. For the sake of caring about some change, I discover I must ignore others. I can manage concern over the fire signal in a small town, but the same noise every three seconds in Chicago iced me.

Limits were shadowing morality for me: I refused the questions of this or that, them or these, clarity and principle, precisely because

I couldn't face limits. Expediency and pragmatism are big systems in this culture: We raise our children on them. They allow the illusion of later, of expansive time. We'd get it right later. For now, just get it done.

Later is gone. Later is now. I'm living my everlasting life this afternoon. The appointment with principle is one I would prefer not to miss. Such tardiness is inappropriate.

Maybe we even have to age inappropriately to do it well. While allowing some things to slip, the lesser, we hope, we will have to dust off indifference for the larger matters. Like who we care about and how we care for them. Like who gets to step on arthritic toes and who doesn't. Surely there will be more threats to keeping our spines firm than osteoporosis. The merchants had no intention of leaving the temple until Jesus threw them out.

4
darts in
the vestment

CALL

darts in the vestment

CALL

THE LUCKIEST THING that ever happened to me is that I became a minister. A woman minister they call me. Seventeen years into it, I'm ready to drop the adjective. So are most of the people I know.

It was sheer luck. I was married then to my first husband, and he was dodging the draft in 1969. One of the more honorable ways of doing that was to go to seminary. The Rockefeller brothers, then, picked up the tab if you were one of those people who hadn't considered the ministry before. My husband qualified as a biologist, so off we went to seminary. The first woman professor at the University of Chicago Divinity School was then recruiting women. Her strategy was to recruit the wives of admitted students. When she called to invite me, my response was simple. It beat working as a secretary to put him through school. It never occurred to me that all the things I did for free should be educated, or credentialed, or salaried. Good ears, good shoulders, the ability to organize and evoke, capacity to care: all these things came with the territory of being female. Or so I thought then and may still.

I loved every minute of divinity school, and he hated it. Two years into the course there, I recall vividly one of my professors asking me to sit down after class. I did. He inquired as to my plans following graduation. I told him I planned to be a parish pastor. He said, "Sit down." I said, "I am sitting down." He said, "Don't you know that the Lutherans don't ordain women?" My response came from a distant part of my gut. How could that be true? The church of my childhood, which I loved much more than I knew, didn't ordain women? Impossible. The church was too good to do something unfair like that. My gut still calls for a lower GI as I remember the shock. It was the loss of innocence toward the one thing I thought of as good. Here I was getting more hooked on religion all the time, just as it was about to throw me for a loop.

The Missouri Synod Lutherans of my youth gave me an extraordinary parochial school education. They did "open classroom" before they realized they were against that sort of thing. Twenty kids in four grades per room. Two male teachers who stayed forever and had the ethnic certainties of Germans with NO questions asked about the certainties of any other ethnic tradition, which is to say they had a good solid hatred of Catholics. This was later invalidated thoroughly by their religious teachings. They taught the three R's but each was secondary to the two hours of daily religion in which the readable parts of the Bible were all memorized along with Luther's small and large catechism. They had great capacity to turn away their eyes where sexual play was going on in the line to the playground. Good coat closets for the same.

Whenever my father hurt or threatened to hurt my mother, the pastor came. It didn't matter if day or night. The awful loneliness of my mobile adolescence caused in me absolute dependence on the Luther League. Through the church Youth Group I at least knew one face before the terrifying opening day. In college my father threatened to punch out the campus chaplain for encouraging my attendance at the Washington Peace March. Moral defense was my greatest need in the late sixties, and the same church that bred in me respect for authority stood with me through disrespect. How could my great protector, the one thing more sure and continuous than either parents or home, be opposed to my service?

The spiritual orphanage I sometimes inhabit began that day with the professor's unwanted unwelcoming. There were some hilarious moments as the church tried to get rid of me without saying why. They never could quite come out and say the reason was my gender. For a while it was the non-denominational seminary that I attended. That's when they sent me back to a Lutheran seminary for ten courses in Lutheran tradition. Then I couldn't get a "call" — which means both a job and something religious — because I wasn't Lutheran enough. As they were recommending another year at another Lutheran seminary, to relutheranize the pagan, feminist, activist who my 1972 person was, I was walking around in a daze. Not Lutheran enough? Grandparents just off the boat, attending services in German language at 8 a.m. at Immanuel Lutheran

Church. Parents German Lutheran, baptism at eight days. Lutheran parochial school. Luther League up the wazoo. Lutheran College. Married a nice German Lutheran boy whose mother spoke to mine in German. Not Lutheran enough for what? I did manage to arrive exactly twenty-four hours late for the ordination exam that they consented to give me. Not that I was feeling ambivalence or anything. (They had never mentioned grades as the issue. I had excelled in every school I ever attended.)

Other times were not so funny. I really didn't understand discrimination. My father had coached me out of it, literally by teaching me sports. First, softball, where on the team he coached I became a state champion pitcher, then basketball, but always more subtly by treating me as the son he must have wanted. I wasn't treated as a girl at home, and therefore couldn't understand the treatment of women outside. My choice to "follow" my first husband came from deeper messages: what my mother had done and what all my friends were doing.

The same luck that got me into seminary got ordination for women. Let's define luck as pressure combined with position. Churches would never have considered ordaining women in our current numbers if it hadn't been for the women's movement in the larger society. Pressure was everywhere. "We will embarrass you." "We will call you a bad name." My position, ironically, following my husband to freedom as credentials portray it, made me be one of the first women to request Lutheran ordination. Such a prominence I never would have forecast in my wildest imagination. But by then I was having to do what I had to do and say what I had to say.

I was not eloquent. First I had to say it wasn't fair. Then I had to keep going, through all the bad jokes about gender, through the obscene scrutiny, through the misery of losing my faith while having to tell everyone how strong it was. Finally I had to leave the church of my youth, knowing that I would never go back. Today I marvel at how long it took me to leave. It took me two full years after seminary. By then, I wanted to go to their party even less than they wanted me there. Today I marvel at how I begged them for work, begged them for permission, begged to be a part of their club. I would not do that today. But the twenty-three-year-old woman is rarely as clear as the woman of forty.

My departure happened like this. We moved to Tucson, Arizona, again, for my husband to continue his schooling. I did all the things the Bishop there and then wanted of me. He then informed me that there was no way any church in Arizona was going to ordain a woman, no matter what the national church said or didn't say about it. After five years of seminary and a Lutheran (of course) internship for one year, I was starting to need a regular job.

Churches call jobs for ministers a call. The language is good. Women, like men, could be ordained if they could find a call. Unlike men, we could not find one. Very few churches were "ready" to have a woman pastor. Just as I was about to take a job at the Garibaldi Employment Agency in Tucson, as a counselor, because, after all, we had eaten tuna fish for four solid months, I had a thoroughly female brainstorm. It must be my clothes. I bought an entire new outfit, with jewelry, at the department store where I had a credit card, donned it, knowing it might have to go back, if poverty continued, and I then proceeded to knock on the door of every church in Tucson. I said to them that I wanted them to give me a chance. "I have two degrees, excellent references, and a strong heart. If you will hire me as an associate for half what you should pay one, I'll wager you that you'll want to keep me around here." I made this speech to the Methodists, Presbyterians, Baptists, Congregationalists, and the Disciples. They were all amused. Everyone, First, Second, and Third, turned me down.

Back to Garibaldi's, until I remembered that the minister at the First Congregational Church had been half interested. I waited in his outer office and struck up a conversation with a woman who was also waiting. He was in conference. (Now I know what that means.) Her name is Winifred Johnson. She is now eighty and bedridden. She is the reason my luck held. Pressure and position reappear. I told her my tale of woe. She said, "Come with me." We went in to see the minister when he was free, and she informed him that the church would be hiring me and that she would personally guarantee the money. Two months later her lover of forty years died, and thus my first funeral was for a lesbian couple to whom I owed more than I could ever imagine.

For two years I worked at the Congregational Church in Tucson, making a lot of silly mistakes, learning a lot, being happily employed but always assuming the Lutherans would repent of their foolish ways. They didn't. Finally the people at First Church said, "We want to ordain you." It came just like a call is supposed to come. It was an invitation. That acceptance, after all the rejection, graced me and allowed me to stop staring at and pounding on closed doors. Of course, I felt guilty leaving the Lutherans. How could I reject them? I have known many Catholics who feel the same way: the church kicks them out because they're divorced, and then they feel guilty for leaving.

The ordination itself was pretty weird. Thirty men laying hands on my head. That was the first moment I really felt that thing called sexism. I remember getting very bummed out about there being no women in the laying on of hands. Everyone else was getting giddy about the so-called sign of the double rainbow that appeared in the Tucson sky that very afternoon. That piece of luck was not the true story. The true story was that Congregationalists are not very different from Lutherans. They are just friendlier.

From Tucson I went to Philadelphia to work on a staff as urban minister with a Presbyterian United Church of Christ congregation. From there I went to Yale to be an associate chaplain. By this time I was already bored with the press releases about the "first woman." They had the same rhythm as those reports of the first man on the moon. I knew the only reason I went to Yale was because my college chaplain was the senior chaplain there, and he liked me. He was not just looking to emboss his staff with the feminine. In each of these first three jobs, I was in a "team" ministry. I know I'm supposed to be good at teamwork, being a woman and all, but I'm not. I really wanted my own church.

After being rejected by a series of churches that no man with my age or experience would have even considered, I was called by the First Congregational Church in Amherst to be its senior pastor. Amherst was the first time in eight years of ministry that I felt like

I was doing the thing I had gone to seminary to learn. I preached every Sunday, and buried whoever died, not just the ones the senior minister didn't want to.

The whole range of ministry was mine, and I liked every second of it. Every silly quarrel with the organist, every nuance of poinsettia and lily placement, the Sunday School curricula and the meetings, meetings, meetings. There was something so bureaucratic about being the associate pastor and something so domestic about being the solo. Now it was my job to go in the night and break up domestic quarrels, to do for other families what had been done for my own. I spent the days dying with the dying, holding their hands, stroking their hair, not on assignment from the boss but because they were all my people. Associate ministers are encouraged, probably with good reason, to focus on the congregations' second-class citizens, either the young, or the old, or the community. I never believed in team ministry, I guess, and of late have become quite convinced that three hundred or so is just the right number for a congregation. It's enough to support one but not two clergy. As soon as there are two, more time is spent in staff meetings than in work.

I was happier than I had ever been in Amherst. The congregation seemed to come to life before my very eyes. One Christmas Eve, the twenty or so residents of the shelter we had in the church, after refusing many invitations to worship because they "didn't have the right clothes," marched to a front pew because it was the only one left. There wasn't a dry eye in the Inn. In a land as deeply divided as this one, such border-crossings are both rare and glorious.

Of course it was gratifying that the people in Amherst were willing to open their beautiful building to the poor. It almost blocked the disappointment I felt when three of our members voted against rent control in the town meeting. All that's really been possible in my ministry is to bring the haves into contact with the have-nots. To meet, to touch, to know. That's my only experience with hearts going from hard to compassionate. That Christmas Eve was a meltdown.

The people in Amherst probably didn't know which part of me

bothered them the most. At first they were divided: Was it my gender or the fact that I had just divorced? Before they had enough time to resolve that conundrum, I remarried, this time to a Jew. Some would say three strikes; the people in Amherst didn't. I'll remember their welcome to me for a long time.

I think it was the negative effect of affirmative action that caused me to leave Amherst abruptly for a job in Chicago as an executive director. The Chicago folks felt pressure to hire a woman and somehow picked me. A brief breakdown in my luck. I'm glad they wanted a woman but wish it could have been someone other than me. I loved Amherst; the congregation seemed alert to the gospel; the holier spirits were amassed. I was censoring less and less of my preaching. I was newly remarried, and the congregation was behaving like a human being to that enigma. I was carrying Isaac, my first born, and deeply happy. But these people from Chicago kept calling, wanting me to be their founding director for a new center to prepare clergy in a new way. I took the bait, fully agreeing that new preparation was required but forgetting what the Lutherans had taught me so well about the devil.

Old teachers don't want new teachers around; they get mad as the devil when one comes along. Thus for four years I endured the testosterone poisoning of a fifty-three-member, all-male board of directors, lost my base in a local congregation, worshipped in a different house every Sunday, and this time nearly lost my faith for good. The one thing I have in common with Jesus is that I can't stay out of trouble with the religious authorities. I despise them in fact and hate what they've done to religion. They've put it in their pockets, snuffed out its light. They tried to perform the same operation on me.

Let me tell you what happened when my twins were born. Yes, two years after Isaac came Katie and Jacob. They were born about five weeks early and Jacob required the many-tubed trauma of intensive care. I had worked until the day they came and had negotiated a maternity leave of six months in which I would work half-time for the same salary. My board was very generous with money. But, as I lay in bed with Katie, while stumbling downstairs to see Jacob, I kept thinking that any minute the phone would ring or a card would arrive. For seven days in the hospital I waited for some comment from a member of my board. None came. I had plenty of visitors, and plenty of calls, and plenty of flowers, from friends, family, my husband's board, students, secretaries, babysitters, and neighbors. In fact, during this very stay, I became aware of just how vital the network of women clergy from around the country is. After many political struggles, we have formed a bond such that long-distance phone calls overwhelmed. I could barely get any rest. But the local neglect really hurt.

It was then that I gave up on the big religious systems, then that I realized what at my own peril I had forgotten. Big systems hurt small places. My board consisted of the seminary presidents, bishops, and presiding officers of Protestantism in Chicago. They had forgotten how to rejoice at birth. They didn't know how to take care of the sick. They were too busy defending the status quo against the spirits. One of the bigger mistakes I've made in my life was to leave the vitality of Amherst to move ''up'' to this position. I rue the day I chose to work with the Pharisees.

I made my way back to a parish, this one on eastern Long Island, with none of Amherst's literati to sophisticate religion. Again three hundred members. Again we are happy. I feel more secure when I am dealing with the people of no cloth. They frighten me less than the Pharisees.

The clergy actually remind me of cholesterol. Fatty deposits. I'm sure that's because they always want to have breakfasts, so ''busy'' are they. There is something out of whack about the clergy, out of time, or out of place, like a body that takes in too much and stores what it doesn't really need. In my youth I met clergy I was able to love; since I've been an adult, it has become harder and harder to tolerate them/us.

The anti-clericalism began in earnest when some women from a neighboring congregation made it clear that their minister was sexually harassing them. ''Suck my dick for a sign of forgiveness.'' I don't make these things up. Then it became clear that none of them really helped the strangers who came to their doors. On more than one occasion, I've had to put up their homeless.

Two causes of this malaise in what could be one of the better professions are psychology and professionalism. Maybe these things are the same. Somehow the lost status of clergy has caused us to grub for credentials, to become more professional when we should be trying to be less so. Thus we actually imitate psychologists with special training and secret languages, distance-making, and closed doors on our confidential offices. We give up so much for these imitations of the modern healers. We give up the chance for communities to take care of themselves rather than hiring experts. We hoard the power to heal rather than spreading it around. We individualize what is collective. The failure of a marriage is not psychological; it is more religious and economic as an experience, then political and personal. The biblical notion of covenant embraces all these complexities; the psychological notion of "marriage counseling" closes the door on too many worlds.

We have mostly imitated the psychologists on our road to becoming more professional. But we are happy with any lead toward it. We prefer to buy our own house rather than living in the parsonage. We pile degrees on top of each other. We go to workshops in church growth and "management" as though congregations were to be managed. Supposedly, however, our authority is from God through people. If we don't trust that, who will?

What pleases me so about the ministry is the distinctiveness of the vocabulary. The language has a rhythm that the world has lost. It is anti-technical, relying on the mistakes of one married couple to issue in forgiveness for another. It is progressive without having to demean the past. "Behold, I am doing a new thing; now it springs forth, do you not perceive it?" (*Isaiah 43.19a*). It relies on the common senses of seeing and hearing, first wanting to know our capabilities of doing either. It has an odd sense of time, relying on the future to better the past. It has a populist urge, making even God as human in the Christian version. It has a ritualizing, binding effect, making more sense of our development than K through 12. We move instead through a series of rituals from baptism through confirmation to burial.

The gospel indicates that the poor carry a blessing, that small is large, and large is small, that things are not the way they're advertised. Mountains and valleys substitute for the flat one-dimensionality of our fatty existences. Why do we eat so much bread that does not satisfy? Manger, miracle, myth, magic, or danger and deliverance, or home and homelessness, time and timelessness, strangers and sojourners, exiles, the importance of being off the beaten track, these all become our vocabulary.

I know I was called so vigorously to Chicago because I had used these languages creatively. My preparation in seminary in the late sixties was in a different Chicago, one not yet cemented in its own famous past. There I was required to learn close to the poor, to live in their shelters and eat their soup. Whatever romance I had had about them was already lost. Saul Alinsky had taught some of us a little course in community organization that had deadened forever the lure of credentialed therapies. The goodness of those times still flickers; it remains the capacity for opposition that I have left.

There have been many good fights. We fought the State of Massachusetts as it tried to dump six million dollars on western Massachusetts for "real" shelters. That is shelters with paid staff and rules where real people like my congregants are no longer needed and are thus kept from either the face or the blessing of the poor. We bought a defunct taxi company with a community-church coalition and turned it into a worker-cooperative until the state ruled that it was illegal not to make a profit on cab service in Connecticut. We organized women transit riders in Philadelphia into a group to take back the night. Day after day we toured big-wigs into open closets in the subways where women were pushed before they were raped. We trained hundreds of women in rape crisis counseling so that women would not have to rely on institutions for healing words. We fought the state of Arizona for refusing food stamps. We did income taxes for people who couldn't read.

Mostly the big systems won. But one triumph of the small over the large happened in that income tax clinic. A member of my church was a school principal and enough of a do-gooder to sign up on Saturdays to assist the poor with their taxes. He worked with a Mexican woman who happened to clean the office of the dentist who was his next door neighbor. She told him how much she made. It was much less than minimum wage. Of course he had to say something to his neighbor about this matter. His words were eloquent and contained the proper mixture of judgment and forgiveness. Strangers really can't do either.

Every one of these words (Alinsky would have called them all actions) depended on staying close to the victim. The Bible never says the word "poor"; the proper translation for that word is "the oppressed poor." It makes it very clear where Jesus stands: with the hungry, the sick, and the lame. So few people have the chance to be blessed as daily and as fully as a minister who can speak these languages.

Or clobbered. I had a habit of adopting at least one transient in each of my situations. You can't refer everybody, and I really didn't believe in referring anybody. Thus it was that Owen hit me over the head with a hammer one Christmas Eve. Imagine me explaining to the officer that the drunk in question did live with me, that these were his first drinks in eighteen months, that I was a chaplain at Yale, and that the mauve velvet dress I was wearing had nothing to do with either. I was off duty. With the exception of this one terrifying incident, Owen was a remarkable housemate. For years he did all the housework, refusing a penny, all for the sake of being with a family.

The real problem with professionalism is that, in the name of avoiding risks like Owen's hammer, it refuses the opportunity to help. Relationship is what helps people, and relationship requires risk. The main way I've found to bypass "professionalism" and its pet, "psychology," is to refuse to refer people. I require the congregation to enter into relationship with them instead. I also refuse to counsel people. I refuse that distance. I give them the chance to hit me on the head or in the heart. Sometimes they take that chance, but, more often, they take their own risk and care back when care is offered.

No one requires that clergy behave like junior shrinks. We go to that safety zone all by ourselves. Upward mobility is a temptation for us as much as everyone else. Perhaps women have it easier here. For us ordination is already upward mobility in status terms. For white men it is downward, especially now with so many women in the profession. For women it remains a compliment to be called "too masculine"; for men "too feminine" is not the same. Thus money loss and status loss join gender loss to make men easy prey for temptations. Women have it easier here. The reason I love the ministry is this very mix of gender. If one is too masculine and the other too feminine, does that not constitute confirming data for the androgeny of it all? If one actually wants an integration of these roles, rather than a theory for same, there is no better work.

Not to mention the flex-time, the decent pay, the exposure to difference in age and class and race, the sheer satisfaction of being present to so much of the world as it marches by. We know about AIDS before the first broadcast on it. Neither our news or relationships require filters: We're sitting on a front-row seat on what many think of as life. Only the barbers, and the beauticians, and bartenders have it better.

For me seminary meant not having to decide for graduate school in English, drama, or creative writing, or social work, or business administration. I got to do all of them with one degree. What other job can start a day with a dozen twelve year olds who are finishing an overnight, go do a burial for an eighty year old, discuss a wedding with two starry-eyed people, visit a murderer in jail, and end with a party where all the "young" couples are discussing when they took marijuana and which female enjoyed which part of the male revue attended the previous night? People do not exclude clergy anymore from these things, thank God.

None of these privileges would be mine if the women's movement hadn't come along to say out loud what I thought was already guaranteed. Women ministers are redundancies. Our gender matters very little. The whole business of being pioneers gets in the way of assessing the real agenda. That agenda has more to do with ministry and less to do with women. We'll now have to see which of our mighty words will pass the test of middle age. What of the mess we inherited dare we "fix"? What of the mess did we make

by our own overpopulation and overdoneness? Now that I am a
religious professional (ha), I take these questions very seriously.

Will women clergy have to better their male peers? I seem to
think differently every few weeks. This pioneer generation of women
clergy is so littered with inter-generational conflict between forty
year olds and thirty year olds. These women are as different from
each other as they are from men. The younger ones are so grateful
for their jobs; the older still angry at the fight they endured. We'd
better wait a while longer before taking on our male peers; for now
we have each other to understand.

I have learned that we know very little about God; neither Father
nor Mother is an adequate notion. I have learned that it is possible
to do harm as well as good, and sometimes, especially, to do harm
while trying to do good. The whole conundrum of hope rests here.
For what dare we hope? To abolish racism? Not until the victims
show us the way. To surpass our parents' achievements? Only if
income is the criteria and only then if adjusted by inflation, both
the material and spiritual kind. To convince the world that sixties
youth are different, better, unique? That seems so silly now.

Luck ran its course long ago on my ministry. Now I'm here
because there's nowhere else I want to be. I'm here because the
questions have become so interesting. I'm here because any young
women or young men, who are influenced by me in the complex
ways I have been influenced by others, deserve the benefit of my
musings, not as accidental moments when sexism is announced
but as one of the things we prepare for in adult life. Not a vague
intention to accept a call if one happens by but ears to the ground
listening hard.

Don't tell my ordination committees, but I'm not sure that I've
yet heard my call. Too many voices. Cacophony. Too many
"women" filters on ministry questions. Too many Pharisees and
too many professionals. Certainly too many would-be shrinks. One
of the best things I've done was to challenge the new practice of
psychological testing for the clergy. My challenge was a total flop,
with just about everybody deciding I was nuts. Or at least severely
wounded by an authority problem. Precisely. I thought the authority

to call was with God through people. That people had the authority to lay on hands. If instead of weeding out bad clergy through congregational vote, we now pay psychologists to do it, what will that do to the muscles of a congregation's authority? What has it already done?

Oh, well. My ears are to the ground. I really never know what I'm going to hear until I hear it. The Bible is perfect in these matters: Let those who have ears hear (*Mark 4.23, Revelation 3.6, Luke 8.8*). Let. Permission. Invitation? The luck to hear it when it comes.

A call is both a job and something religious. I've had a great job, and now I'm looking for the religion. All the other religion I've known has sneaked up on me from behind. Unawares. Surely this will too. Always before I've found the hand of God in luck, in a combination of pressure and position, time and space. Here we go again.

5
bleeding hearts
and open doors

POVERTY

bleeding hearts
and open doors
POVERTY

It HAPPENED AGAIN yesterday. I was using an illustration in the sermon about Central America. "Those bullets," I said, "those Contra bullets that shot the pregnant woman weren't paid for by my withholding. No, that must have been someone else's withholding." The sarcasm was intentional. The tears were not.

The only other time I've cried preaching had the same geography. Romeo's death. Obviously grief remains over the long-distance damage we did to the Vietnamese. Why else would I lose distance when the pain is so far away? Why bother crying about the poor anyway? Talk about a waste of time.

By now I've been called a bleeding heart often enough to get a bleeding ulcer. Accused of caring wrongly so often, I have adopted a bit of an armor. I care meanly, fiercely, clumsily. The real reason care has become so cold, however, is not the accusations of my political opponents. The real reason is that I really don't like poor people.

My so-called ministry with the poor is not tender, or gentle, or even kind. It has had most of its softness stripped away. Confronted with a request for assistance, I never yield until at least three nasty questions are asked. How did you get yourself into this mess? How are you going to get yourself out of this mess? And who, besides me and God, is going to help you? I then invite the stranger to worship and start telling him or her just how much help our congregation needs. We are desperate for their leadership and participation. They don't believe me, but it is true.

What the poor do in our congregations is to keep the arteries in our eyes from hardening. They allow us to hear the gospel. Without them and their persistent threatening presence, we would long ago have all lost our common senses. Fortunately the gospel only promises that we will be blessed by the poor. They are walking beatitudes. It does not promise that we will love them or them us.

One of the reasons they are so poor in the first place is that the way they are unlovable (like the way we have of being unlovable) has been exposed too often. Their whining powerlessness evokes the whining powerlessness in us all, and particularly so in their myriad "workers" who invade their privacy so frequently.

The poor remind us of powerlessness, ours to help them, theirs to help themselves. The size and strength of the opposition to the poor, some of which is inside the poor and most of which is outside of them, is the devil's doing. No one else takes responsibility for it, that's for sure, not them, not us, not their workers, not the government, not even God. Powerlessness blesses but only after all the excuses have been exhausted.

People call these blessings "church mice" which labeling always makes for a perfect liberal spat. Liberals hate having their class show. They/we hate exposure. When language exposes as much as "church mice" does, the paternalism and maternalism slips down below the outer garment. One is embarrassed but not deeply.

Shallow embarrassment permits the use of the name "church mice." One of its meanings that I covet is that of small. At least it's honest. People do think of the poor as little, like children, the poor things that the poor are. Another is their at-homeness in places like churches. Surely the "church mice" belong there more than the lords and ladies. They can't be eradicated, short of poison. They sort of come with the furniture. They may not sit on the pews, but they are always there, with us. As Jesus said, always with us, scaring us when we come upon them unawares.

No, this language is not flattering. It will embarrass you to tears, deepening what began as shallow, because through it we may glimpse just how harshly we feel about the poor. When they come close, through the red doors of our church buildings, let's say, the tears disappear because they have to. We cry about Nicaragua and Vietnam; we have to talk to America. In that conversation with the visiting beatitudes, we find ourselves exposed. Our helplessness talks to theirs, which is one way of describing a good relationship or a good blessing. They arrive when all the excuses have been exhausted.

When my husband asks me what kind of day it's been, I often joke with the reply that they put the sign out. The fictional sign is "Free milk and cookies at the Congregational Church." That's my best answer why some days will be full of blessing and others just full of excuses. I really don't know why or how the "church mice" gather. They just do. The head of a local welfare agency told me once that if you start giving these people good service, they'll just want more. I heard him loud and clear. Even a little encouragement goes a long way.

One may tell another that the big red doors are open. But probably they don't because they don't speak to each other. The only way they happen to meet is by waiting together for an appointment. They come by themselves and leave by themselves. One showed up on Labor Day and was crying in the sanctuary because she had lost her lover. Since a previous holiday visitor had threatened to hang herself in the sanctuary, much attention was paid to this newcomer who turned out to be quite capable of taking care of herself. Another came with seven children, all under the age of eight. Fortunately, she brought a baby sitter. But none of them had a place to stay.

One came with a grandson, all the way from California by bus, to finish her college education at the university. She was fifty-eight years old, he was six. All their possessions were in plastic bags, and her dress was ripped in three places. But that didn't mean she was torn. When she sang spirituals, more than music came out. Then, when he told stories, everyone listened. They managed in Amherst until the cold sent them back West to family and sunshine. On New Year's Day they boarded a bus, having sold everything to pay their way.

They shared the kitchen for the summer with another family from the West. This one had two children and a mother. They had been sleeping in their van in the parking lot. The black California family and the white California family had homelessness in common but never did agree on how to clean up the kitchen after they made their separate meals.

Those in families seem to manage better than those without.

The seventeen year old, who came right after she lost her job at Pizza Hut, left a lot behind: a warrant for her arrest, a lot of earrings, a few unfinished notebooks from the last time she went to school, a wallet, and a teddy bear. The only person who looked for her was an insurance salesman. All he was willing to say was that she was in a lot of trouble. Her things, all but the teddy bear, are in plastic bags with her name on them. (Also ready to claim at any time with proper identification are the Iranian student's books.)

The eighteen year old with the broken ankle had also lost her job. She said she had a boyfriend, but he didn't want to meet her at the hospital during the blizzard when she went there to miscarry. He admitted to being her boyfriend but had little else to say. Fortunately, the police could get through the snow, and so they got her to the hospital. Before that cold escapade she had been wearing a sock over her cast in the snow while looking for a job. The Survival Center was able to put an end to that. Once she said she had to have money to get a "prescription." The total bill was seventy-six dollars.

He was also eighteen, came from Denver, purported to be in "big trouble" with the National Basketball Association. He never mentioned what the trouble was and got up every morning at five to wash the floors at a local grocery store. That was one of his three part-time jobs. On Christmas Day he ate alone, walked alone, and neither took or made phone calls. On the fifteenth of July he simply left town.

The Department of Defense just the other day made a personal call to inquire of another. They said he was applying for a job and that they needed to verify his address. But he had none when he came and left none when he left.

Many of them have done time at the Northampton State Hospital before its liberal decision to liberate the mentally ill. Some want to go back; others healthily hate it. Some fall in love and wonder if they can "take" getting married. Others simply float. Many try to do volunteer work and get their volunteer positions by avoiding any mention of their past.

One came in saying she couldn't stand to go to parties. She had a job, an apartment, and a boyfriend. But she couldn't stand crowds. They caused her to sweat, become speechless, and to vomit. It turned out that she, like many, was raped by her father. Another has nightmares for the same reasons. Incest is a hard word to say, like rape used to be.

Another called from Holyoke talking about Thorazine. When all was said and done he needed forty dollars to pay the rent, or the old man was going to throw him out. Again.

A family of four came one Saturday night. Someone in Ohio had told them that there were jobs here. And so they had driven through the night and were exhilarated at arriving. He looked for three solid days for work to support his wife and babies. We gave him the gas money to go home.

Writers and poets show up frequently. They admit less readily that they are broke or homeless or crazy for the day. One tried to sell poetry, a dollar a poem. We bought forty. She went all the way to Boston to fight welfare for her rent subsidy. I drove her there and on the way back brought her brother. The rest of the weekend was spent with her landlady, who was tougher than the tenant, the police, the brother, and the son-nephew. Family reunions are not always happy.

One was a truck driver and wanted prayers for truck drivers. Many simply want to call their relatives. Others want jobs working for peace. One, at age sixty-seven, told a life story that made her current problem seem minor. Her husband had died just as her baby was born, and so she had worked in Santa Fe and Atlanta for ''fancy ladies'' and now couldn't get along with one of her relatives. What she wanted was someone to call her relative to get a few things straightened out.

These descriptions don't include the regulars: Alcoholics Anonymous on Wednesday, Saturday, and Sunday nights; Over-eaters Anonymous on Sundays. The doors see both the peddlers of new solutions and the persistence of old ones. Some even have solutions larger than the problems, like the man who did unauthorized fund-raising for the Emergency Shelter and pocketed the donations.

The doors also see a lot of disappointment with the church. One claimed to have been raped by her minister in Texas. Another claimed that the priest was a drunk. The child made his own appointment. He said he tried to talk to his last minister about what he had done wrong to make his parents get divorced and what he could do to bring them back together. Being only ten at the time of this consultation, he was a bit small for the chair he was sitting in.

A local travel agency is still trying to collect the bill from someone imported last year from Honduras. It's a long story but the man said his mother was dying, and he had to get his sister here and could we help. He even said he had a job and gave a lot of guarantees, all of which were checked. Then he disappeared, and the immigration officials are still looking for all of them.

She came from one of those fundamentalist groups. Actually several came together in a blow-up of one highly authoritarian collective. Some found life in the free world manageable; others immediately took on substitute tyrants.

Those who want to go to the newspapers with their story tend to have a point. If you lose your apartment (eviction, non-payment of rent, bad relationships with your neighbors or their dog, whatever) and if you don't have an address, then you can't get your welfare check. If you can't get your welfare check, because you don't have an address, then you can't keep your children, because if you're on welfare and you can't get your welfare check because you don't have an address, then you can't have your children. Best solution of course is to stay where you are. But if that doesn't happen, trouble becomes capital letters TROUBLE. Catch-22 ties you up in a braid. Now that the Emergency Shelter is here, you can use that address for the five days you are there, welfare can send you the check and if it arrives, and you've already gone, you can go back and pick it up.

Sounds silly but it helps. Because if your teenage daughter has ''gone bad'' and caused you enough trouble to get you thrown out of your apartment, you can live at a camping spot long after the season is over. And your two younger children can be taken away as soon as you miss your welfare check because you don't have an address and camp won't work.

Even the Youth Center had had enough of this one. He stole from us (a shovel and a pillow, which he also returned), allegedly stole from another local church, and then figured out how to get a place to stay: in jail for four months. Stealing a car almost always works. Now he's out and says his parole officer can't find him a job. He needed money to pay his mother back the twenty-five dollars she loaned him. When asked if that were true, his mother responded, ''It's only twenty dollars. He's trying to make an extra five bucks off you.'' Before the problem with the car, he spent most of the winter in the lounge, interspersed by short trips to Brattleboro to see his girlfriend. He had a terrible cold and needed a mother with at least cough drops. But Mom had no cough drops for him.

Parents come looking for kids they can't find. They have photographs. They tell stories. They say, invariably, it's not their fault before they leave, eyes glancing from left to right in the nooks and crannies, seeking something they can't find.

Among the regular so-called ''church mice'' is one who washes out her stockings in the sink and sets them out to dry. This practice has yet to make church committees happy. Another hides behind the dossal curtains and when asked what she is doing there replies, ''Nothing.'' A third (unknown) makes a small habit of stealing wallets from the office. For a while two of them received messages on the phone. That's stopped since we sniffed a drug deal. Who wouldn't when every other message was ''your car is ready''?

The members of the support group for unemployed persons are significantly different than most of these isolated hoboes. They, at least, have the sense to seek each other out. Like the one who tells about the personnel officer who told her never to admit that she didn't have a job when looking for a job. Thanks a lot for the advice. Another tells of the time she offered to work for half salary. And a third reports that she is three weeks into joblessness and has yet, as an alcoholic, to have a drink. Small potatoes, some would say.

One called one night to say she was jumping off the bridge. She didn't because (a) she was too drunk to get there, and (b) life, all things considered, was more precious than joblessness was terrifying.

Another said he had dislocated his shoulder and thus could not work. The lady who had been keeping him had decided not to any longer. He wanted to work, so we gave him a paintbrush. But he couldn't risk his body to paint that might have lead in it, or so he told our bemused custodian, who went on to paint the room with the paint that had no lead in it.

One called to ask if the baby could be baptized even if the parents weren't married. The answer to that question was yes, but it would have been no if they had also asked permission to have a full-blown domestic battle minutes before the service.

Most who want to wed come from outside the congregation. They come in through the red doors out of an ancient call to involve the church they've forgotten long ago in their lives. Many involve an ex-Catholic who has more assumptions than Carter has liver pills about the church. Most these days are second marriages. One wedding stands out because the bride's parents didn't show up. She handled it fairly well, but the groom flipped out, followed soon by his parents. Another time only a few of the invited guests showed up. And, once, the groom showed up sufficiently in his cups to warrant a postponement. These weddings are so much in the minority that the red doors, on the whole, are happy to see the long absent walk through.

The lonely come in just to talk. And the elderly stop by on something that appears to be an errand but may be an innocent ruse. And many bring items to sell in the furniture exchange, ranging from their own largesse all the way to their grandmother's silver or imported brocade from the old country. We hear enough stories directly without having to eavesdrop on items in the furniture exchange. People come with stories about how their husband is doing them wrong, their children are on drugs, their second teenage daughter is pregnant, or their aging parent is driving them crazy. There are also the problems of sickness and death, but these things happen to everyone.

All that is unique about the "church mice" is their special story of their special problem. Not all abused women react the same way to abuse. Not all poor people deal with poverty the same, nor does every homeless person fall into a pattern. What the chemistry is that makes some cope, and others not, some to hide behind curtains, and others to call the newspapers, some to steal cars, and others to sing spirituals as a response is anyone's guess.

The red doors don't pretend to have a theory of why. It's not always poverty, not always injustice, not always the sins of the parents visited on the third and fourth generations. Sometimes the responsibility is personal, other times social. Sometimes it's sheer orneriness or laziness. And sometimes bad luck gets in league with bad timing.

But in the majority of the cases the special story results from some larger circumstance. The problem comes from the incest or the joblessness, though we are rarely privileged to see economic problems or psychological problems alone. They love to get together and link up and make a mess of things. Most get knocked over by these circumstances, and every now and then one doesn't.

Some even use their trouble as a school for feelings of entitlement. They begin to believe that someone owes them a living. Thus they don't like the rules at the Shelter, which require getting in by 9 p.m. and out by 9 a.m. They learn to trust less and less and to con more and more. The difference between fact and fiction fades.

Charles Dickens was the last person to think that the poor are pleasant. Not everyone who comes through the big red doors is looking for a free ride and its quiet humiliation. Some manage to avoid the sense of entitlement and its ''con'' of themselves and the people they encounter. Some still believe in grace and hope that there's yet a place on earth where they may be at home.

One of the poorest people who ever came gave fifty dollars to the church. And a while back we received a payment on a loan made over five years ago. The Cambodian family whom the church sponsored in June just grew one of the best gardens around and has been most generous with their produce. And every Sunday morning at ten the members roll in, in numbers strong enough to withstand the ''church mice'' of the night and the week. What the members give goes out. Every time the pastor's discretionary fund has emptied, someone has died or lived to fill it. There's a story about that in the Bible, about the woman and her jar of oil and how it doesn't empty because she keeps spilling it around (*I Kings 17.8-16*). The jar doesn't stay full by protecting itself from the unpleasantries of the poor.

Through the doors also come stories of sexual harassment in high places, impotence in sex and life, daughters who live with men where parents don't approve, people who don't get tenure, and people whose parents both die in a month. But the difference in these latter stories is that someone besides the teller cares about what's going to happen next. Trouble in community is a whole different thing than trouble in isolation. Hoboes have trouble that has no place to go. Maybe that's why it comes through the red doors.

My point is simple. If you see big red doors and don't bow a little in their direction, you're missing out big. All preachers are not like Jerry Falwell or Jimmy Swaggart. All congregations are not like the one where your mother sent you to Hebrew or Sunday School. All "church mice" are not small. Some don't even like government cheese. Big systems are often big systems of stereotypes; small places can change them.

Furthermore, people don't spend enough time on their knees at the right altars. In religion that is NOT trapped by culture, "church mice" of all economic sizes find a place to make and touch meaning, to affect the world that affects them so much, to give and not just get, to enjoy a gladiolus or two. They get to relax, to take risks and be supported, to be quiet and think, to eat good food with good friends, all with free child care on the premises. They also get to sing and be happy in a group that is not drunk. (Most of the time.)

These blessings are not segregated. The poor come no less than the rich for these "hand-outs," these freebies. The rich come no less than the poor either. There is an extraordinary equality to the urgency for grace.

It would be false not to note the pain in keeping the doors open. Tired clergy. Spirit-tired. Congregations who think the minister is their private nurse and therefore shouldn't waste time on the other mice. "Church mice" themselves who are a pain in the neck.

Being called a bleeding heart only hurts the first hundred times. After that you get used to it. Not every time I dare to care do I get burned. Just often enough to keep the bleeding ulcer diagnosis a possibility. A bleeding heart doesn't know when to quit. It's fear of blindness that keeps me going. I might miss something beautiful. My despair might be proven wrong. A bruised reed God will not break, nor a burning wick quench (*Isaiah 42.3a*). Ordinary promises yield ordinary responses. They don't move us to tears much — or even embarrassment — just to get up in the morning and go open the red doors.

6
curves
in the road

SPIRIT

curves
in the road
SPIRIT

Some people get in the car, drive straight to the super-highway, and get on it. These same people get places on time, they live within their budgets, and they are in the broadest and best sense of the word, dependable. Other people get in the car, go about five miles on the interstate, get totally bored, and take the first exit, sure that they'll find a better or at least more interesting way, and arrive, almost predictably, fourteen hours later than they said they would. One road is straight and simple: on it the map works. The other road is curvy and complex. The map is a humorous addition to the adventure.

We drive our cars on interstates; we live our lives on backroads. Even the people with the more orderly lives get detoured. Things get curvy no matter how hard we try to keep them straight. It is on the curves and the back roads that most of us find God. On the superhighway we are too preoccupied with our destination to enjoy the journey. God is a journeyer. When we are journeying, we have a better chance at finding God.

I know these things are true because of a lifelong immersion in the Scripture. It has been my bath water, my background, my mother tongue. I am one of those immigrants to the modern world, come from the primitive, with echoes of promise and possibility disharmonizing with production and processes at every turn. There are a lot of us. In our youth we heard so much about God that we thought we had a bellyful. We stopped listening. We listened to other songs, other certainties. Then the road got curvy, and we were forced to consider once again the possibilities of the spiritual life. The journey. The journey with God.

Our grandmothers read the *Upper Room* every day, learned its verse, took in its morality, prayed its prayer and felt satisfied. The gods were placated. At the end of each two-month period, they got another pamphlet from the church, and sometimes they paid for it and sometimes they didn't. The discipline of daily devotions came with doing the wash on Monday. That's the way the royal "we" of simpler times did things, and because all the others ordered their life in this way, we did also. Why bother asking a lot of stupid questions?

There are days when I am so lustful for the orderly life of my grandmother Ella that I forget how miserable she was. I forget the bottle she kept under the sink after Grandpa died, how naughty she could be in saying "bullshit" to my mother, how compulsively correct she had to be, how full of Milky Way bribes her refrigerator was, how grabbily she handed out nickels and dollars for kisses. I forget the side effects of her order. The house was too clean. The recycling done too much in earnest. The hatred of sex too sincere. She even hung the clothes angrily on the line. On Mondays, of course.

Back and forth go the curves in the road. In the winter she wore a mink coat in church. In its pockets were Life Savers. In exchange for being quiet, we got Life Savers. It was bliss. But so was dancing wildly the first time in church. Making noise and lots of it. No candies to silence us now. Beyond the bribes, looking for God. Beyond warm mink in which to snuggle, too.

Too much of what I know about God I learned from this grandmother. She, of course, hated God. God was the source of her misery, her pathetic need to do everything right and everything on time. She was scared to death almost every day of her life and barely had the courage or energy to emerge. But emerge she did, talking German when she wanted to protect herself, talking English when she wanted to boss someone around. God to her was mean. If she behaved, God wouldn't hurt her too much. If she didn't, the curses would fly.

Being rowdy was one way to evoke a curse. Being dirty another. I'll never forget the day of my first marriage. My whole family was staying at her house. Probably we did that to enjoy the pain of it. Or maybe we had the wedding in her church and stayed at her house so as to avoid the pain of another choice — her pain, that is, not ours. She had a way of being extremely loud about her pain.

A friend of mine arrived early and presented his relatively well-shaven person at the door for her inspection. It was 1968. She allowed him in, sat him down, offered him a wrapped hard candy from the bowl on the table. He took one. You never disobeyed my grandmother. He proceeded to unwrap it, and she escorted him physically to the kitchen. ''No unwrapped candy in the living room.''

My mother had been prophesying something akin to a religious experience right before the wedding. After all her wedding had been so blasted, why not mine? The trouble would be about sex. Ella would try to tell me I wasn't going to like sex. I got the message but remembered that I also didn't read *Upper Room* or do the laundry on Mondays. Maybe my sex life had a chance that her gods didn't give her. At the time I was much more concerned about my sex life than my spiritual life. Too few curves in the road. Too much satisfaction at the altars of 1968, godless as they proved to be.

My other grandmother, Lena, everyone said was godless. She gambled, she rarely did laundry, and she had no money or candy with which to bribe. She laughed a lot and placated no one, not even the gods. They say she used to go to church, but when I was growing up, on Sunday mornings, she was usually sobering up my step-grandfather, her second husband, a plumber who drank too much on weekdays too. Generally she was kind to his addiction, although she was also famous for making him sleep on the hammock outside if her generosity was too frequently abused. When you were around Lena, you could pretty much count on having a good time. Food would appear. Beer would appear. Stories would stack up, and time of the clock variety would disappear. Lena died coming back from a Bingo game. She was hit by the bus that carried her home. I'll never forget how sad I was when they woke me up in the middle of the night to tell me. Joy might disappear with her. When Ella died, I had a very hard time locating grief. With her gone, I had a feeling that the joy and the spirit she had been so good at sweeping out of the house might sneak back in.

Lena did one thing for my spiritual life that proved worthy as a clue to God. She took me to New York City, on the bus, and walked me through Chinatown and Harlem. She was very brisk about it. "Look," she said. "Smell," she said. "You need to know that some people are very poor." Because of her tour I've had no reason to forget that. Thus initiated, the blessings of the poor were a possibility for me. Ella was always pretty sure that the poor deserved to be poor and that the more distance we made between them and us, the better. There can be no doubt that there are many different forms of impoverishment.

Having these two very different grandmothers led me to one of the more interesting questions. How did one of these achieve such a right relationship with God and the other one such a wrong one? How did one make so many happy and the other make so many sad? How was it that Lena never said anything about God and yet knew peace and joy, while Ella pillared the church and was miserable? Did church make Ella hate God?

Neither could be accused of success at achieving right relationship with God. Not even Lena was perfect in her peace. She had anger seizures, not sex seizures. Her blood pressure was appropriately high for a woman with little, whose husband was belittling that. Ella crooned the hymns but hated God. She also hated life and was glad for the good case of nerves such hostility bequeathed her. The nerves allowed her to "be blue" without having to take responsibility for the blueness. But Lena at least seemed happy, seemed like she was leaning on something besides her own resources. She stood up straight when people crossed her rather than digesting the pain hungrily. She laughed a lot. She gambled vigorously. Laughter, courage, chances — these strike me as the marks of God in a way that cleanliness and quietness never will. Lena wouldn't be caught dead on a superhighway, and Ella wouldn't be caught dead off one. Did following the instructions make Ella hate God?

Clearly too much of what we know about God comes by way of inheritance. With the bath water. If the water is poisoned, we are poisoned. If the water is clean, we are clean.

All I really know of God is partnership, a sense that the way I am going is the way God would have me go, that this decision and that response and this accepted consequence are not mine alone, but partnership with the God of my birth and bath. My spirituality — how I hate that word — my faith is that I am not alone, even when I take the wrong turn. That I will not be abandoned, even if I persist in the wrong turn. That God will enjoy me and my journey. That there are things that are expected of me. It's not just me and God, but God and people, and I'm one of God's people. The covenant of God may actually be with the land first and with people second: my faith is that I am part owner in that pact. I am a participant, a landholder, one with a claim. I enjoy participation in creation with God, even if the creation is just a broccoli timbale. I laugh with the God who makes space for my peace and my joy; I hate the God who bosses me around and asks me to be miserable. Both of these Gods are present in my spirit.

When the mean God invades, I become dry and dusty, a desert wanderer who has no place to drink beer or tell stories. I buy manuals on spirituality as though I could buy gusto at the book store. I follow the instructions. I improve my rituals. I "take time" for God as though God weren't at the computer with me now or eating timbales with me later. I have discovered that God isn't too big on command performances. We have that in common.

On the other hand if I don't allot time during a day to meditate, or breathe, or think, or walk, or otherwise shake the busyness from my soul, God evaporates in a different way. God becomes too much timbale and too much computer and too little God's own whatever. Person? Being? Breath? I have discovered that God isn't too big on me setting the whole agenda for our relationship. Time to be open to the thoughts the clock won't allow is crucial. Ritualized time. Time that no one else can have, not even me. Without this time that is given away — back to God, like the tithe goes back and can never be given — without this time, the rest of time becomes chaotic. God is pushed out of the calendar, off the agenda, and the me who journeys alone takes over.

Now, she is a bitch if there ever was one. She can make my grandmother's controlling personality look like cooperation. Our biggest idols are always ourselves, or so I have discovered when

I forget to communicate with my partner. Jesus makes a big deal out of the difference between the water and the spirit. I think that means that any ritual becomes plain water. We can pretend to be with God but actually be journeying alone. We can go ahead alone and discover that God catches up with us anyway and wants to turn us back or around. Without time each day — legalistically, orderly, or fanatically — to discover what's happening on the way, we'll never know. We'll die dumb about our own lives. We should know this from reading the Bible, but book learning doesn't take. We have to find out as we go.

I found out most about rebirth and renewal by my failures to achieve it. For the longest time I wanted to quit smoking. I quit smoking so many times I think I set the world record. Elaborate ritual. Much prayer. Extraordinary support systems. And repeated failure. I also wanted to get over the pain of the breakup of my first marriage very badly. Again extensive prayer, and counseling, and ritual, and failure. In each case the harder I tried to get on with my life, the harder I fell. My efforts were counterproductive. The best advice I got was from a dear friend who told me that the suffering would end when it was ready to end and not before. Ouch. "Like a Pollyanna," she said to me, "you will just wake one morning, and you'll discover that you are ready to go forward from this divorce. Then you will start forward. Until then you have to muddle and circle and dive and dwindle." I hated her for saying that. She was nevertheless absolutely right. Vows and good intentions are water; rebirth is water and the spirit. Rebirth comes when good intentions are met by God on the road.

Most of us, most of the time, are so hostage to our desperation for renewal (or change, or cessation of addiction, or peace) that we miss the rebirth the road offers. We miss either the stranger, or the interruption, or the book that is carrying God's spirit. We miss the song that might lift our hearts just high enough to allow the spirit a breakthrough. The radio may be humming, we are rarely listening. We are hostage to our need for renewal, so hostage that we program it. Almost any human being can give you a long list of needed self-improvements, starting with health continuing through attitude, not excluding the family budget, the overflowing closets, and the disgusting cellar. Most people have at least one seriously broken relationship that they are carrying perpetually in their suitcase. The spirit is either whispering or screaming, "lay your burdens down," but, so loud is our desperation, we can't hear. Many of us have more than one broken heart or at least enough hurt to make us suspicious of love and its highly vaunted solutions to life's problems.

We have tried many mechanical methods of rebirth. Counseling. Prayer, after prayer, after prayer. Yanking our own bootstrings. Kicking ourselves in the butts. Megavitamin therapy. Fasting. Effort, after effort, after effort, until failure is our middle name. Clearly the United States has spent millions of dollars on the scar of racism. We ran a war against poverty once. We have attended thousands of seminars. Many of us have read thousands of words on these subjects, and spoken thousands of words on these subjects, and risked friendships over these subjects, and FAILED to accomplish much healing, if any at all. We are not novices on racism, or broken hearts, or unhealthy habits. We are waiting to be met on the road of our efforts. We are desperate to die to the old self. We are waiting for our homesickness to turn into pilgrimage. We want to get on with our life, get on down the road.

Rebirth is a vow to change met by God on the road. It is our effort to be different, plus God's blessing of that effort. Rebirth is homesickness turned forward into pilgrimage. Metanoia. Conversion. The weather changes in our soul. It is a new day. Suffering is the travail, the labor pain, the whole creation groaning, and us with it, and it with us.

For me, the journey has taught that moments of conversion are more possible when I stop trying to make them happen. When the effort ceases and the burdens are laid down. When I vow that I can both take the pain, when God's will not mine is done, and when I'm not just conning God to get me out of the mess I'm in. Conversion comes not as a result of my efforts but as a result of my willingness to drift in effortlessness for a while. Rebirth may be when we take all the lostness and whimpering on the road, and all the hurt along the way, and all the failure that striving has taught us, and we declare it part of the journey. Homesickness turns pilgrimage here, when we declare the suffering, also, part of the journey and not just the joy. When burning out becomes ours and not an invasion. Some wise people call this the time when we say what we've learned from our trouble. What is it teaching us? Who did it make us? What gifts did it carry in its wake?

Of course these moments take a long time in coming. They begin as interruptions of the good stuff we have in mind for ourselves, and they linger on as the genuine journey. Sometimes we are not even alert to the fact that these shifts are occurring. Particularly if we have forgotten to pay attention to what is going on, if we have spent too much time pedaling and too little time pursuing, we may be completely unaware of the visitations of the angels. We may hang on to our old home even if it has been refused to us. We may refuse new homes that are offered to us. Rebirth is not guaranteed. It is just possible. Always possible. Turn away from homesickness, if you can; but if you can't, let it be part of the journey, part of the trouble you need to slog through to be you.

Trouble is on the main road, not the detour. At our most troubled, and our most homesick, and our most burnt out, we are still on our way. God is still traveling with us, begging us to be partners, begging us to be people who know how to spot the spirit along the way. The best definition of the gospel message I ever heard is that the gospel is the permission and command to enter difficulty with hope. Permission. Command. Difficulty with hope. Not ouchless but not all pain either.

The journey confirms the gospel. People report miracles when they let go; they report the multiplication of trouble when they hang on. Women meet men they can love just as soon as they give up on ever finding one. I know: That's how I met my husband. Mothers and daughters find strength to struggle together rather than estranged once they say out loud that this relationship may never get better. When we give trouble a name, say out loud our part in it, often, as the great spiritual sages of all time have said, when we let go, let be, stop fighting the existence of the problem, it is precisely then that we meet God on the road. We can have what we can let go of. The very words "I am an alcoholic" constitute liberation in a way that defensiveness never can or will. In these very moments, we meet God on the road. We sniff fresh air. We imagine how good forgiveness will feel. We become capable of talking to our former enemy in new language. The language shifts from the repetition of blame and accusation to the finding of shared distance and mutual trial. We are not alone. Pilgrimage doesn't guarantee that every relationship is harmonious, it simply puts us back on a main road where we can get on with our life. Even main roads are a little curvy. People used to the easy driving of interstates really need to understand this. The goal of renewal is not easy driving, not that awful promise "freedom from stress." The goal of renewal is new capacity: It is freedom *for* stress.

We are more capable of rebirth when we ritualize our readiness for it. When we get good at waiting. When we expect God at every curve, even when God hasn't shown up for any in a long time. Horizon watching. Expectant walking. It is absolutely no accident that every other psalm is on the theme of waiting. Isaiah's fundamental eloquence is on the subject of waiting: "They who wait for the Lord shall renew their strength, they shall mount up with wings like eagles, they shall run and not be weary, they shall walk and not faint" (*Isaiah 40.31*).

We are more capable of renewal when we are journeying, when we are on the way, when we value now time more than later time, when we have faced into the trouble on the main road and not anxiously dumped it off into the weeds on the side. We are most capable of renewal when we stop aiming straight for it, compulsively, angrily, nail biting, and bitching all the way about how, with the kids in the back seat of every car, "We're never going to get there." We'll get there in God's good time and not a minute before.

We are least ready for renewal when we follow instructions and do things everybody else's way but our own. When we are obeying social orders, day in and day out, God gets squeezed out. We ourselves get squeezed out by making everyone else's agenda our own. My grandmother Ella was so scared that someone might disapprove of her that she never gave them a chance to love her. They would only love her if they identified with the trouble on the road, if they saw in one of her curves one of their own. Her clean house was only going to drive them away. It is no accident that she was so mad at everyone else all the time, while smiling, of course. She was mad because everybody was making her do things everyone else wanted so as to avoid genuine contact with them. Walking all by yourself through a whole life is very sorrowful. It makes you angry. Probably even God gets tired of angry people after a while. They make lousy partners on the journey.

Staying on superhighways for too long can also prohibit renewal. They are just as boring as they look. The emphasis on speed, on "getting there," on arriving are perfect partners for the upward mobility that has become our modern version of the Apostles' Creed and Declaration of Independence rolled into one. It's not that God is anti-product or anti-progress or even opposed to getting there; rather God is so much less interested in these things than most of us are that we become strangers while walking along. God is more attuned to what's happening on the way, to the sights and sounds of partnership, the ripples of water viewed with extravagant praise. These, like making love, for God, are given all the time they need to be properly appreciated. How we felt or thought today is interesting. Not how we will feel in the next grade of condominium or once we have a summer place. The future is interesting and better futures are ideal pursuits. Hurrying toward them, however, is a God-blocker.

When we make the mistake of liking Georgia O'Keeffe's excellence more than ordinary, daily excellences, we begin to break with God. We become driven, not drivers. If we begin to like only O'Keeffe's excellence, and to pursue it greedily and hastily, we drive God away. Once we have mocked and made an enemy of God, the possibilities for renewal, for change, for capacity to withstand the curves — those now, and those coming — evaporate. Once that happens, we are condemned to excellence. We are condemned to fast forward. It is in this hell that violence develops: The source of powerlessness is in these repeated choices to speed along the main road, fervently trying to become more important than we need to be. The speed is inappropriate. Burnout joins violence as consequence. We get old fast precisely because we are going too fast to recognize our youth as it and we pass. The partnership with God is antidote to these disenfranchisements. Maybe it will turn out that ''spirituality'' begins when we get a speeding ticket, when either violence, or poverty, or burnout, or loss of our deserved home announces that we are going much too fast.

Right here we see one of the chief ways that good news can come out of bad. The very reflection on the sources of violence, or poverty, or homelessness, or fatigue permits reflection on God. Getting a speeding ticket is no fun. Being warned can be deeply embarrassing. And yet these signs may be of God. They may be one way our partner has of notifying us that something is amiss in the pattern of our journey. Systemic evil is an announcement that something is wrong. Many hear that announcement as personal judgment and go belly-up in passivity. What can I do about it anyway? Others listen more deeply and make the connections that are obvious. We live in a way that makes violence a necessary consequence. We lose power on the way. We live in a way that makes fatigue a necessary consequence. We get tired going so fast. We live in a way that allows some to be hungry and others to be on constant diets. We are shamed by such facts. These are warnings, they are announcements, they are reminders that God is not mocked. Time to reflect on these mysteries, each and every one of them, is essential to the soul. The very reflection on bad things — rather than avoiding them — deepens wisdom in us and makes us capable for the journey. The very avoidance that we practice, as though these things were not a part of the journey, as though they either didn't really happen or if they did they certainly have nothing to do with our lives, this very avoidance over time threatens to destroy our soul.

Consider David's grief over Absalom. The watchman advances with good tidings. He makes a noisy entry. King David has won his kingdom. His enemies are roundly defeated. At each restatement of the good tidings, the king asks, ''Where is Absalom?'' Finally the messenger tells him. Absalom's courage on the battlefield won the war. "Absalom is dead." David says what any father knows is true. "Would that I had died instead of you, O Absalom, my son, my son!" (*2 Samuel 18.33*).

Good mixes it up with evil. Victory mixes it up with defeat. Are not our upward mobilities always so? Isn't it great to get a little closer to Georgia O'Keeffe's status? And, is there not always, inevitably, loss involved? Proper grief is important to the journey. It is as important as proper joy. The only implied curse in the New Testament is the one in which Jesus queries what profits a person if he or she gains the whole world and loses their own soul in the process (*Mark 8.36*). Loss is part of gain, and the wiser spirits suffer their way to this knowledge while the weaker ones, by ignoring loss and speeding ahead, suffer all the time.

When people beg for reasons about why things happen, they often accuse God. God gets accused every day all day long for not sending the proper signs. Bad weather. Innocent suffering. Putting a father in the hospital a week before he's to walk his precious daughter down the aisle. Foul-ups of every variety. These are laid at the feet of a puzzled God by an angry public. Only a fool would not identify with this angry public. My grandmother Ella is not the only one mad at God. It's hard to go far down the road and not pick up a few rocks to throw. Enough bad stuff happens for which no one can be blamed. Cancer and AIDS lead the pack, I think, although pollution-caused disease, which cancer may actually be, is sure to be in competition soon. Why can't we just die of old age? Why does there have to be so much pain involved?

A seventy-three year old woman explained to me last week that her now-deceased husband had only three wishes. He wanted to die at home, he wanted to live to be eighty, and he wanted to celebrate their fiftieth anniversary together. I thought these wishes were absolutely elegant, so lacking in the standard megalomania of the times were they, so refreshingly relational, so achievable. She said he got two of the three, and with that a tear of joy came across her face. He died in the hospital. To want something so ordinary and to have it denied. This is cruelty, God, and you know it. If you know it, why don't you do something about it?

The poet Auden tells us that nothing can be loved too much, but that everything can be loved in the wrong way. Fortunately the man who died in the hospital wanted a parlor death, but from what I could tell, he didn't want it in the wrong way. He wanted God's will just an inch more than his own desires. That struck me as appropriate. That took the edge off the cruelty. It allowed the last curve in his road to make a kind of sense that otherwise could have allowed that curve to be the one that threw him. Why, at eighty, should anyone open themselves to such a loss? By then, is it not our job to reflect sufficiently to include suffering and surprise in the daily calendar? I can't imagine anything more important that we might be doing on the road.

For most people, of course, these weighty subjects of violence, and death, and poverty are too big to get through the door. For most people, thirty days of mega-muggy weather can initiate a journey for the spirit. Kids who refuse more than thirty times to pick up their socks, or dogs with unconquerable fleas, or cars with non-functioning mufflers are often enough to kick off the existentials. Life can be cruel in its daily barrage of duty and obligation. You know this, God. If you know it, why don't you do something about it?

From our culture we get constant good advice about how to manage the daily round of dullness. Hang tough, hang loose, hang in there. There is no doubt in the common wisdom that hanging is important. From God the advice is much less about hanging and more about walking. Look carefully where you walk. Look carefully while you walk. I dare not make too much out of the difference between these two verbs, but the temptation is too strong not to point out that culture's word is passive and the gospel's word is active. Hang reminds me too much of fingernails. Of course there is effort involved, modestly, but mostly the attention is to the tree or the rope on which we are hung. Walk evokes the partner. Walk means movement, eyes open, feet working, and pace is the weightiest matter.

> How fast can or should you go?
> What do you see along the way?
> Who do you walk with?

Factor in both the heavy and light troubles of human existence to those three questions, and both dullness and cruelty turn immediately interesting. At the proper pace, with the proper partner, there is plenty of time to do all the dull time-wasters. At the proper pace, with the proper partner, there is plenty to see along the way, plenty of both cancer and courage, plenty of lights burning out and plenty of lights turning on. Absalom is dying while David is winning: Some are weeping and some are rejoicing, and this is going on all the time, off the superhighway on the back roads. Sometimes the best thing for an aggrieved spirit is to be in touch with an Other who will point out the existence of other worlds, other possibilities. Surely Ella needed Lena to take her to Bingo once in a while, and Lena needed Ella to instill a little fear. We can all issue speeding tickets to each other. The partnership that makes the road good is not just human-divine. Like the way good has with evil and evil with good, it is the very mixtures that are significant. It is on the journey that we find our way.

7
the senile
old woman

CHURCH

the senile
old woman
CHURCH

I DIDN'T WANT to visit the senile old woman. The only possible interest in the occasion was sure to be how she misconstrued the past. She might remember that I was the pastor and not the head of the women's auxiliary. She might consider her recently deceased son dead, and then again she might not. Although she had attended the funeral in the front row, she recently had taken the position of living twenty years ago in a time when he was alive and she was beautiful.

Thus I would sit in the tired old easy chair, drawing in the faded elegance of her living room. I would count the knobs on the cherry chest and again assure myself that one was missing. I would contemplate the oriental rugs scattered properly about and sort of hope that she would not trip on them again.

Like so many of her disposition, she would not mind dying. Her most genuine questions are reserved to the question of the gods' purposes in leaving her around for so long. She knows she is finished but puts up on an engaging costume to cover the truth.

Fortunately her past is quite dramatic. She was an actress. She divorced her literary husband early on and retained a magnificent friendship with him. The two of them, though living apart for most of their adult life, huddled close at the funeral of their son. She walked in, stately, on his arm. Now, instead of talking about the present, when she can no longer quite manage New York City and its life, she regales with "her writing." Just the mention of the writing gives permission to a long story of youth or adolescence. There is nothing wrong with the stories whatsoever, except possibly their veracity.

She could do better. She was educated in the finer places. She enjoyed most of the fun that life offers. There is a bright twinkle in her eye. She is still able to talk about the "boys." Her grand-daughter thinks this subject is overworked. I think it is a miracle at eighty-five to live alone and to be horny.

My best evidence for her spunk came when she went to the hospital, having hurt her back by falling, probably on one of those elegant, inefficient rugs. There she refused to wear clothes to bed. She had not worn clothes to bed for most of her life. Why, she asked the nurses, should she do so now? I simply delight at the thought of big nurse and her minions having to answer that question. Since senility had not caused her to cease her habit of sleeping during the day and being awake at night, the hospital had other reasons not to enjoy her visit.

Despite my respect for her moderate but interesting grasp of reality, I did not want to sit there that day. I had heard most of the stories before, it was after lunch, the repetition was sure to put me to sleep. My dozing, I think, she would notice.

I needed an amusement, a way to engage at the proper intervals, and I got just what I needed — the fantasy that Gladys was a good metaphor for the church in the late twentieth century.

Lost glory. Improbable. Still capable of standing up to big nurses and big systems if unlikely to do so frequently. Not easy to stereotype. Repetitive. Deeply in need of a new look, a new take, otherwise destined to put you straight to sleep. Sexist in an unintentional way. And deeply bemused about whether the Son of God is alive or dead.

The bread on my table is bought by the church; I work for it the same way other people work for General Electric or the Transit Authority. Most of my security as a person comes from the church. In my youth it was the church who saved me time and again from various serious temptations to be a jerk. In my adulthood, when my face was shoved in the bowl of *isms* that are true about my nation, it was the church that caught my fall into total cynicism. I am its debtor. It is one of my grandparents; it is Gladys in the risks she took to be her, in the marks she made while living a happy life.

Many would find my problem with the church's senility ungrateful or, at least, marred by too high an expectation. Perhaps it is. Ungrateful and marred, I still expect the church to face facts, to glorify, to stand up to big nurses, to wiggle out of stereotypes, or at the minimum to recognize that women are different now than in previous church time.

If it were only the eighty-five year olds who represented the institution, I could easily tolerate the offense. They have a right to choose their reality, and I doubt if backaches and Pepto-Bismol are worthy of preference. Going back in time and digesting those events less captive to death strikes me as more than legitimate. It is not just the eighty-five year olds who resemble the church. That's the problem.

Real churches have chosen senility over reality. The Catholics autocratically pontificate in ways that change little, no matter how much Thomas Jefferson said about the people and their voice. They seem not to understand the population explosion or the fact that women are no more not going to use birth control than men are not going to drive cars. Cars, by the way, murder nearly as many as abortions. The fundamentalists interpret scripture so literally that we can only assume that they want it not to live or breathe in the twentieth century. I can understand hating the twentieth century. I cannot understand biblical times as a legitimate alternative. The Protestants, with whom I have cast my lot, waffle, and weasel, and jump on the feel-good bandwagon to appease the big nurse of psychology, then jump off and ride with the managers, then jump off and ride with whoever else invites them. We love to be part-ners with culture. Our whoring has not gone unnoticed. People understand this about us and, if they hadn't been so harmed by culture and its rules, they might give us a shake. Since people know, at least at the spiritual level, how harmed they have been by culture's rules, they consider us as less than appealing bedfellows.

The real reason young people don't go to church anymore is they can't find a difference between church, where they might expect to meet God who might be different from culture, and the rules. Catholics obey. Fundamentalists separate. Protestants partner. In each case so-called Christians trade away the capacity to tell culture that there is more to life than moving up. We refuse to engage the realities. If we were senile, we'd have an excuse. We're not senile. We're just turning our head away from painful reality. From a tradi-tion of being the great affirmation, we have become the great denial.

If the Son is alive, or the parent God real, would it not be possi-ble to stare upward mobility in the eye and say "no thanks"? Would it not be possible to face the bosses and suggest that we and our people and our God do not choose to work in ways that demean or harm? Would it not be possible to tell the polluters, authoritatively, to stop and to tell the bomb builders that we don't need bombs? That we have all the security we need by birth and baptism and creation? If the Christ really came to earth to redeem that part of creation that our grandparents way back threw away, would it not be possible to be happy, not worry? "Don't Worry; Be Happy." We need hymns and songs to reassure us.

The real reason I'll probably not be able to continue to get my bread and butter through the Protestant church is that it will die. The institution, like Gladys, will finally be buried along with its distorted past. People who hear the promises of God will not necessarily be sad at the funeral. The churches have been getting in the way of God for a long time, from the time of Jesus when the temple and its sales substituted for the promise of unearned, unpaid-for goodness, until the now of churches uncritically accepting the injuries of capitalism. As if there were nothing the churches could do to stop those injuries, as though God were powerless against the bottom line. Young people refuse church because church has said it is powerless against the bottom line; thus young people simply follow instructions and worship the bottom line. Church is all about what is most important in life. Scripture says it's God, and church says it's culture.

Of course there are mighty exceptions. Black churches in city after city have heard the promise that racism is no match for God. All across Central America we hear reports that God has broken through the landowners system with the message that people who work the land deserve land. And in countless American cities there are para-churches, places where people listen for the words of God and then believe them.

Woman-church is probably the most notorious example. Since so many Roman Catholic women have been told they aren't needed in positions of authority in the church, God has had a fighting chance. These people were insulted by the supposed voice of God. They had to rethink what God was saying and doing in their life.

They couldn't believe that God had no use for them, and they were justifiably ashamed about wanting to ''move up'' in the church structure. The contradiction of that behavior caught them. Thus they were forced outside of the church to look for God. There they found rich blessings in their own gatherings, music that sounded good to the ears, the rebirth of the biblical words, and the rousing presence of the holy spirits.

Non-Catholics haven't been so lucky. We have partnered with the compromises our churches make. We think of ourselves as still trying, searching for balance, as post-modern, if that word means eclectic, mixed up, hungry for diversity and change. We will do better when we die more, when this last generation of mostly older women dies and enough of our pews are empty to remind us that we have fished on the wrong side of the boat.

Just like Gladys, we could do better. We could look more at the present and the nearby future of our much forecasted death. We don't have to live in the past or deny that we are dying. There is a spiritual richness waiting for us Protestants, waiting for us to acknowledge that we are on the way out. The stage of senility we need not prolong. It is a purgatory, a waste of time. Resurrection will follow death. A new church is trying to be born. But most of us aren't even in the throes of labor yet. We are hanging on to our cherry dressers and oriental rugs, wishing with all our might that someone will do something to turn back the clock and restore our lost grandeur.

Some (not all) will have to abandon the old lady and refuse to visit her anymore. She will die alone in her apartment with, hopefully, a cat to keep her warm. They will have to build new houses for the hope of God, speak new words, sing new songs. Maybe woman-church will lead the way. Or house churches. Or consciousness-raising groups or anything small enough and long enough to allow people to cast out all the demons of disappointment from Sunday School and confirmation class and churches that refused them when they divorced or remarried or had relationships outside her narrow boundaries. These new churches may not even call themselves churches. They don't need to. Perhaps they will be spirit sleuths, detectives on the track of the holy: places that allow the void to name the silence, places that begin with the seed of a gathering that knows it is at the wake of the old ways to know God. So many words will have to be spoken. So many people will have so much to say about the damage done to their faith by churches.

After the complaints about what the institutions did to us and to our capacity for God, long after, just like in the rage stage of knowledge of cancer, we will begin to recognize our own parts in the tragic play. We will see our consent. Our flight when we should have fought. Our compromises. Our complicities. We will realize that church couldn't have done all this bad stuff without our help. We will see our partnership in the denials of death. We will remember that we were neither passive nor victimized but rather silent and scared.

There will be mighty words of forgiveness, rushing in from a tormented Spirit. The rooms of the new churches will be washed by tears. People will hold each other up and prepare to struggle toward God, together, alone, any which way they can.

All the spiritual and symbolic starvation of the late twentieth century, once brought to conscious light, will begin to search for food. People will laugh as we read the psalmists' words, repeated, over and over, why do we eat bread that does not satisfy? Why did we eat that bread for so long? The white bread church will fade away as the bounteous table of God is laid out in the soup kitchens of the spiritually homeless.

Whatever this awakening is finally like, we won't know until it happens. It will most resemble that time in our own life when we realize that our parents may have been outrages but that we have to eventually stop blaming them for our life and start living it anyway, even if deprived or constantly hungry for something we're never going to get. These transitions into responsibility for ourselves and away from blaming are no fun, only liberating. They are a walk out of Egypt. So few of us get far enough out of Egypt to know what the routine is like out there that we are going to have to go mapless, unadorned by certainties.

I hope that new churches will meditate on whether or not God survives nuclear disaster. I have been experimenting for years in congregational prayers by praising God by saying, ''Thou whom nothing can destroy, not even nuclear annihilation.'' It often shakes people up. I hear all points of view. ''Yes, God does survive.'' ''No, never.'' It's so much on our minds, at least the unconscious, which I think of as the most spiritual part of ourselves, that minimally we need to start wondering. Is our death God's death?

I hope that new churches will find ways for men to be more like women without being forced into a mold by us or damaged in the ways their expectations have so often damaged us. More properly, the ways we have allowed their expectations to so often damage us. I do hope there won't be priests or pastors but rather abundant leaders, strong, risk-taking, pushy types who will keep shoving everybody out of the Egypts they'll surely go back into at the first scent of genuine freedom.

I'm way too conservative to hope for new liturgies, embodiments, magic, and all the rest, way too nourished by the connections of my own highly normal religious past to want to worship outside of the old lady's cramped apartment. I'd have to give up too much of my childhood to do so, and I feel like life has required that I give up way too much of it already. So I'll be an alert bystander as the new church experiments with new ways to sing and dance and praise.

The reluctance to part with the old stuffier liturgies is probably the real reason I'll continue to visit the old lady rather than participate in a new start. They contain too much memory for me. But the old lady and I will have to quarrel frequently as we stick together. I can't live with senility; it is too boring.

A remarkable thing happened in one of my parishes. A number of feminists agreed that the language we used to describe God was too militaristic, too male, and too old, and therefore they demanded changes. Their demands were to change all the language in all the hymns, prayers, and sermons from being military or male. The words I spoke were easy to change, in fact, I had long ago changed them. The hymns were very difficult, so pervasive was the problem. The congregation studied the issue for a season. Everybody agreed we had to experience the new way before we understood it. So, we changed all the words every Sunday and kept a book at the back of the church where people could make comments. We got some doozies. It is amazing how emotionally attached different people are to different metaphors about God. After all the study, consultation, book reading, and book writing, the congregation voted to authorize a new hymnal. The strategy used in this instance best expresses my compromise between old and new church. The women got a man, a retired pastor with a real gift for language, to rewrite every hymn in the hymnal. Every single one. It took him several years. He researched every one and discovered that most of the hymns had been changed many times in their periods of use. He wrote up little stories about each hymn and he poetically and deftly changed the language to include absolutely lyrical and biblical descriptions of God. (The hymnal now circulates widely and is available through the First Congregational Church in Amherst, Massachusetts.)

The choice to rewrite the old hymns, to do so in the very print and pagination of the old hymnal, to do so lovingly and carefully rather than angrily or meanly, bowed in both directions at once, toward the past and the future. It was a good compromise, a way of keeping a foot ahead and a foot behind without crashing down for lack of balance. I was deeply proud, deeply moved by the whole experience. I used to get nervous when parishioners demanded changes. Boat-rockers and all that. Now I am glad at the arrival of conflict because it means the redistribution of power, some waves on which the Holy Spirit will ride, some good times sure to come right after we get through the hell of fighting.

Because things like this can happen, I keep visiting old ladies in their apartments. I cast my lot with a church that I know will die soon. The protections in such a strategy need to be visible. For me to survive in old church, I need to be clear that I am here waiting for resurrection, waiting to see what God wants to do with the leftovers of one of the most marvelous, if mixed, historical thanksgivings, that of the Christian churches. What's next? Who are we to be now? What's the middle time meant to be? Who will take care of the old ladies if we don't? They are not worthless, nor are they to be abandoned.

I have no illusions about grandeur returning. Clearly the denominations are now doing everything they can to assure and legitimate mediocrity. The denominational structures are more telling of death than anything I know. They busy themselves acting like the world is on their shoulders, fooling no one but themselves that they are harbingers, restorers, or breach walkers. Because many clergy are tricked into thinking they too should move up and work in these structures, a few good people end up being destroyed in them. For the most part, however, those who move up to these structures deserve to be there. Their ear was not to the ground lower down the ladder either, so why worry? The evidence is in: The real life of churches is local, sporadic, hidden from these structures.

I suppose I cast my lot in the old parishes with my ear to the ground for God because of memory, habit, and the faint hope of connections yet to come. I'd love to have the courage for new churches and maybe someday will. There is talk all around of new seminaries and new denominations and new training centers for new types of clergy. I go to more meetings these days than ever before where wonderful people are sticking their ears on the ground to listen for the rumble of the new train. I have no doubts that the rumble will get louder and that we will know, deep within our hungry souls, when it is time to jump on and ride. Until that time, I will bumble along with the old ladies and their friends.

We have at least these choices when it comes to finding God through church. We can start a new formation, a new group, and send up signals that we are on the search. Any of us can do that at any time. Or we can stick it out with our grandparents and beg them to join us on the search for a new day. I keep hoping that some of them at least will come. I had one grandmother who would have and one who wouldn't. Not bad odds.

If we stick it out with the grandparents, stewardship (money-raising day) sermons like the one I gave this year will be necessary. We will have to voice the frustration and hang on to the hope. It is offered here to show one way in old church:

One of James Thurber's great characters announced that the stars had all fallen out of the sky. Many people believed him. "Imagine," they pouted, "all the stars have fallen out of the sky." The hand-wringing continued until they discovered that the man was blind. The stars had gone nowhere. What had fled was his eyesight. Not to know when you can't see anymore is a most dangerous thing. You may have an accident in a car. You may misread your checkbook. And you may, like Thurber's character, misreport. You may take others to darkness with you.

The most interesting thing about the Thurber story is how quickly the sighted believe the unsighted man. They don't bother to look up in the sky and spot the stars. They simply proceed to pout, and wring their hands, and spread the false story about the stars. It is the blind man who must feebly lead them out into the night and press their necks to an upward position. He has to confess his error. "It's not the stars," he tells them, "only my eyes." The sighted crowd quickly fall into another error. They begin to rejoice. "The stars are not gone. Hooray! Hooray!" Only much later do they attend to the personal if singular tragedy of a man who once had eyes who can no longer see. At first the crowd is selfish with the bad news. They can only experience their own loss. Next the crowd is selfish with the good news. They can only experience their own gain.

One of the primary functions of church is that of opposing selfishness. We exist to bring sight to the blind. To help people see beyond the end of their own noses. We exist to bring enough security and confidence to people so that they don't have to believe everything they hear. We exist to remind people that God loves them so much that they need not lean or depend on any other love. No peer pressure, no false prophet, no going with the crowd for those who love God. We can think for ourselves precisely because we are not only thinking for ourselves. We think with and through the mind of God. How would Jesus handle the situation of the man who reports that the stars have gone out? This simple question is ours as people of faith.

Surely Jesus would have considered the possibility of projection, of exactly what happened. He couldn't see the stars. Therefore the stars went out. Jesus would have challenged the blind man to see his own error. He then would have had compassion on the man. Losing sight is a horrible thing. He probably would also have healed him.

A very similar situation developed when we passed our church budget this year. The deacons and trustees had a joint meeting and as meetings go, it could have had a whole lot more jointness. The deacons and trustees were in the same room but not of the same mind. The points of difference were classical, with some people wanting to spend more money, particularly on mission, and others wanting to spend less. If this same conversation had not happened in all the congregations in the country sometime during this fall, and last fall, and all the falls before that, it would be worthy of worry, but since the same conversation happened everywhere, with the same necessity of a few noses going out of joint, it is not worthy of worry. Only notice. Churches exist to combat selfishness. The rightness or wrongness of any one of my own brilliant positions (I did tell you before that all of my positions are brilliant, didn't I?) is only part of the stew here. All of our positions on all issues go into the same pot. They get stirred around. If the Holy Spirit has not yet abandoned us, we come out right where we are supposed to. The budget we finally passed that evening was a good compromise, with a little more money being spent but not as much as the spending faction would have hoped for. The selfishness of our various positions had a little bit more of its hair rubbed off. We had yet another chance to disagree with each other, another chance to learn a little about what it means to be church, which is that we love in and through and beyond difference, that we care about each other especially because we are different. The fact that some of you really can't abide some others of you is a key contributor to our richness as a congregation. We are not all the same here. Some of you are downright obnoxious. Some of me is also downright obnoxious. We are not here to mold each other to our own likeness. We are here to mold each other in the likeness of God. Church is a crucible for caring. We all get bent eventually to its shape. While getting bent to its shape, some of us get very bent out of shape. We will all come here with our own announcement that some stars have gone out. We will all come here with our own story of too much work, not enough support, too few skills, too little time, too little money, too much of bad stuff and too little of good stuff in our lives. We will throw our scarcities and our fears into the pot, and we will hope that enough of Jesus is among us that those scarcities will not be laughed at but rather given compassion, that here we will be recognized for who we are and loved anyway, even if we are blind as a bat and don't really see much of what is going on.

We chose a theme for this year's stewardship campaign and it reflects the compromise very well. The theme was "Do you mind if we try?" "Do you mind if we try to raise this year's budget?" It is a way of recognizing that the budget is larger and the need for increased pledges is significant. I want to draw attention away from the man who couldn't see the stars because he was too caught up in his own viewpoint, and to focus attention on the crowd. Crowds are so easily led. During one of the meetings on the budget someone inevitably said, "We'll never raise that much money." That one statement could have led the entire crowd. It didn't, and it won't because the person agreed to let others try. But its message that the stars are out, that we are an incapable congregation, deserves serious attention.

We know that Jesus and the Holy Spirit are among us because we are able to care enough about each other to forge good compromises. We know that we are a capable congregation because we are giving more food away to the poor. The amounts matter less than our doing so. We know that we are a capable congregation because some of us are caring for the land by political work on the recycling/incineration issue. We know that we are a capable congregation because some of us insisted that the schools talk about racism. We know that we are a capable congregation because our children are learning about God in Sunday School, because our women enjoy remarkable fellowship among each other, because our men are good cooks and, frequently, cheerful workers. We know that we are a capable congregation because we sing hymns together, and pray together, and baptize children, and marry young couples, and bury each other, and because next week we will receive gratefully some nine new members. We don't like it when people, for whatever reasons, whether they be historical or personal or whatever, suggest that we cannot make good on our compromised commitments. Of course all of our commitments are compromised. Our goal is not perfection here. We are not in business just to raise our budget. We are in business to combat selfishness and to promote caring. If we don't raise our budget, it won't be the end of the world. Minot will still run the hot dog stand. Mary will still staff the kitchen. Jim will still yell at the choir. The twelve year olds will still get confirmed. Someone will come along to take Dick's place as supervisor of the sacred things. George will remember early that he has to get ushers for Christmas Day this year. Alice will decorate the church Christmas Eve. Jean and Elsie will still take care of everything that nobody else will bother with. And each of you will make your contribution to this vital community, and it won't just be through your checkbook.

One of our hardest tasks will be to care for each other in such a way as to rout out the pessimism. To care for the pessimists among us. Where does it come from, this sense that our church isn't much, and we aren't much, and other people won't give much? Do you see Thurber's character here, do you see him standing there telling the world about the stars going out but really begging someone to minister to his own loss of sight? Do you see the hidden message of pessimism? Do you know yourself what it is like to live in such an undependable world that you can't count on anybody else, that if the stars are going to shine you have to place them in the sky? What a job. If churches exist to combat selfishness and to promote caring, it is the pessimists whom we will have to take on. It is their pessimism that will throw us all into darkness. It is their loneliness, souls glued to the horror of their own bootstraps, that our ministries will have to consider. What would Jesus do with pessimism and cynicism? He cast the demons out, threw them into the roaring sea. Nothing less is required of us.

We cannot allow people to say that we are not a capable community or that we will never reach our budget. Sure we have a lot of relatively poor people in this congregation. Sure we have a lot of people on fixed incomes. But every study shows that in fact it is poor people who give more, percentage wise, than rich people. A recent study by the Gallup poll shows that people with incomes under $18,000 gave an average of 2.8 percent of their income while people with incomes between fifty and seventy thousand gave an average of 1.5 percent. This statistic is one of the most important figures in modern philanthropy. It means that poorer people give almost twice as much as richer people percentagewise. The widow's mite once again. We must also confront the pessimists with facts. Surely these percentages are paltry, considering the biblical mandate to tithe. A caring congregation would take tithing seriously at least by giving 3 percent to 5 percent to the church and the rest of the 10 percent to other worthy charities.

Stewardship, we will have to tell both the pessimists and the optimists among us, is not so much about these numbers, however, as it is about attitude. Stewardship is the return of blessings. It is the physical sign of caring. When the people give freely and generously, it is a sign that the Holy Spirit is among us, deepening in us the fact that we are not alone, that we do not cause the stars to shine, that we don't have to pull ourselves up by our own bootstraps, that God is with us, and that congregations exist to demonstrate God's presence in the world.

We may or may not reach our budget this year. But we will return our blessings every which way we can. We will promote caring and admonish selfishness. We will combat pessimism.

We may or may not reach our budget but God knows we are a capable community. Jesus is among us, drawing us closer and closer to the crucible of caring, refining our eyesight so that we may more clearly see the stars, which, by the way, at last check, were still up in the sky.

My conclusion, after giving this sermon and hearing the response, was that everyone, including me, is on a search for church, that no one is exempt from the search. We are a little bit at home where we are, inside or outside of religious institutions. We need a place where someone will have compassion on our blindness, where someone will listen to our complaints against the stars, where selfishness will institutionally be combatted and caring institutionally promoted. The big systems win unless the small places are restored or created. We don't create or restore them for the old ladies or for ourselves but rather for both. Both are held by God, both new and old.

8
streets
to dwell in
SYSTEMS

streets
to dwell in
SYSTEMS

"You shall be called the repairer of the breach,
the restorer of streets to dwell in."
—*Isaiah 58.12*

BIG SYSTEMS ENJOY big success by destroying communities. They trick us into thinking that we must fight them as individuals. They trick us into thinking there is nothing but ourselves. As individuals we haven't a prayer against big systems. As communities, big systems haven't a prayer against us.

I think this is how the tricks work. They depend on the illusion of the private. They falsely assume that the frame of experience is individual. If there are bad chemicals in our food, like EDB, we remove the offending cake mixes from our shelves. If a popular movie like *The Day After* dramatizes the consequences of nuclear war, public dialogue reverts to the interesting question of the age at which our children should be permitted to see it. If families have problems raising happy children while making ends meet through the employment of both parents, superwoman erupts as the bearer of that awesome responsibility. If a modern woman can't bring home the bacon and fry it up in a pan, there must be something lacking in her as an individual.

If third generation welfare recipients can't get off welfare, they must be lazy. If a man can't keep a job in a factory, he must be no good. Never mind that the industry moved south. He will retain the sense of individual failure that the illusion of the private permits and encourages.

In each of these examples, public motions cause the trouble. The political economy of food production, of war, of family income, of welfare, and of jobs determines the complex in which individuals flail. They flail to protect their sense of control over their experience, to legitimize the moral posture of individualism. But private solutions won't solve public problems, no matter how much guilt we sacrifice at their altars. Those individuals who attempt to solve their problems privately dare not be surprised when despair is the result of their strivings.

These individuals are out of control. They don't just feel out of control. They are out of control. Robert Bellah's book *The Habits of the Heart* tells story after story of the way this individualism replaces both religious and republican values in the contemporary American consciousness. His partners in research demonstrate the extent to which that private morality, what I code as the "it's all up to me" syndrome, has grown and taken over the minds of community organizers, businessmen, and housewives. To me, the most telling story in the book was of the man who inherited his used car business from his father and yet insisted on the myth that he was a self-made man. The morality is so strong that we use it to flatter ourselves — or guilt-trip ourselves — no matter what the reality.

The privatizing of individualism is oppressive both ways. It is oppressive because it flatters our "accomplishments" excessively and judges our "failures" unjustly. I can think of nothing sadder than "it's all up to me." There is no basis from which to thank our parents or our children for their gifts to our lives. There is no room to hold a public accountable for the wars to which it may invite us or the economic dislocations that may occur.

The subject of the *it*, of what *it* is that is all up to me, requires some disclosure. As far as I can tell, *it* is upward mobility. The goodness presumed in our system, our freedom, is that of getting our slice, our private sanctuary in city or suburb. Mike Royko almost won the contest for the motto of New York City when he recommended "Where's Mine?" Should any reader find this analysis exaggerated, I recommend that you choose the liberal arts or community college of your choice and sit in their student lounge for an afternoon and eavesdrop. Students today are quite clear about their expectations of the *it*. They have no need to dress up or over their desires for upward mobility, so weak are the restraints against *it*.

Surely there remain those who limply dance to a different drummer. Their limpness is understood: The other tune is now so loud, the alternatives so faint. Only privatism would dare expect heroics on their part against such clear instructions and penalties from the system.

System is a word used intentionally as a complaint, and I want to elaborate on it. By *system* I mean only the interaction of the parts. *System* is a word we use too often to excuse passivity. Here I want to acknowledge that systems could also have parts that interact positively, as in a community of individuals, but that in our current usage, *system* means something large and alien over which we have no control. It owns us rather than we owning it.

Privatism is one of many systems. It falsely assumes that it is all up to me. And that your life is all up to you. It falsely takes credit and lays blame. It also functions in a third way as dark glasses — to prohibit understanding. It also refuses to account for positive public initiatives. In this country enormous good, as well as evil, has been accomplished by publics working together. The public health movements, polio vaccine, social security, national parks, land-grant colleges, and civil rights legislation join thousands of local initiatives through community organizations and developments to tell a rival tale of the good that publics remain capable of. Those who ridicule big government and who hurt themselves by keeping government off their backs refuse to praise when praise is due, so powerful is the ideology of private morality.

There is the constant anxiety surrounding upward mobility — will I or won't I make it on my own? In addition, there are resulting penalties to relationships. Moving up often means moving away. Moving up requires choices against family, friends, and place. Uprooted on the average of once every five years, Americans probably say more good-byes than anyone on the earth. Now that the economy has dictated that both men and women work outside the home, we have even said good-bye to the nurturing of our children. Surely under these parenting arrangements, they will be more self-reliant. Grandparents were kissed good-bye long ago by upward mobility, and friends are clearly a luxury we can only afford in those brief moments in high school and college when we are not making grades to get ahead of our friends.

These internal shadows that darken upward mobility have external consequences as well. We get to be both anxious and lonely AND to cause trouble to others whom we don't even know. Freedom to be me is so important to Americans that we must enforce it in Central America. The lessons of Vietnam, like so many others, receive the customary blindness. Freedom for certain classes and races in America is so important that we dare not let everyone have it. Big government with loads of regulations is just fine for the poor. If they had a check rather than services, God only knows what they would do with the money. Freedom may be all important for certain groups of Americans, but they don't believe it enough to stay out of other people's business. Freedom all too frequently requires the control of others, strangers like communists or blacks or browns or yellows. Individualism does not even carry respect for other individuals in its moral wake.

In biblical terms, the measure of both a person and a community is treatment of strangers. When freedom for me to make it becomes too important, others, sometimes even friends and family, become expendable. As individual freedom becomes the apex of a value system, strangers are in danger.

The passivity toward community and its forms of living, which develops when activity on behalf of selves is so all consuming, clears a wide path for the big systems to do with us as they will. It encourages voting percentages of 50 percent, doctors who feel quite free not to discuss our health with us, lawyers on whom we depend for solutions to neighborhood and domestic quarrels, ministers to whom we charge our spiritual health and then criticize when they don't preach ''good'' sermons, teachers who are responsible for putting learning on a spoon, and so on. We become so accustomed to giving our public life to experts that we give them more and more control over our private life too. Now we can't even handle our own grief: A grief specialist is needed. As individuals and communities, in our idolatrous pursuit of individual good only, we have given away almost all our power. Our powers include healing, mediating, worshipping, and teaching. If the community can't teach its off-spring how to raise its own children, how can a six-week workshop at the local hospital expect to? Political passivity has invited an army of experts to take over the tasks that individuals in communities could enjoy.

Two examples of how I have given away power recently should suffice. My neighbor was a non-drinking alcoholic. One summer night I heard him talking loudly in a drunken stupor. I pretended not to know and then pretended for his season off the wagon that I didn't know. The friendship that we had established, which included significant conversation about his drinking times, had weakened, and his wife endured the new season alone. Why didn't I get involved? Because I obviously chose my freedom over our friendship. It was my loss.

Another friend of mine had brought her dying mother home from the nursing "home." She did this against the doctor's orders, and she was afraid. Had I been able to organize our little circle to help her with food (remember the covered dish), time off from nursing, or even a steady dose of encouragement, we would have enjoyed the community of the non-medical society. I discover that working women lose these opportunities frequently. We have followed the instructions of a feminism co-opted, one that told us to reach for our individual gusto, just like men. It never occurred to the privatized feminism that if men could become more like women, rather than women becoming more like men, that everyone could gain. Everyone could stand a double dose of nurturing in this society. These are our losses and the systems' gains.

If the harm that big systems do to small people in small places were limited to the neighborhood or friendship level, maybe that wouldn't be so bad. The harm is not thus limited. Our lack of participation with each other paves the way for larger and more frightening idolatries. They are more frightening because they invoke the question of scale and size. They become a peculiar form of American totalism or totalitarianism. We feel guilty not moving up; it *must* be our fault if we are poor. It is so invisible that most of us, including me, feel naughty even mentioning it. That we have permitted such concentrations to develop in a nation founded on a democratic distribution of power is almost too much to bear. It seems absurd or paranoid, yet I am afraid that I see the contours quite clearly and daily. They beg me eight or nine times a day to see them, but I resist because of the shame and powerlessness I carry toward them. Note with me how deeply ironic it is that in the name of protecting the individual we have made her and him so very ashamed. Trying to get large has made us small; trying to be small enlarges.

The size of the system became most visible to me when I became involved in a community development project in New Haven, Connecticut, many years ago. Briefly, the cab company was bought by a group of churches and individuals to become a worker-owned, not-for-profit, employment-creating service. The previous owner had milked the company for tax purposes, and there were almost no cabs on the street, much less jobs. The costs of cabs were to be lower than the going rate so that those who really needed the service, that is, people who couldn't afford cars, would benefit slightly. It seemed like an everybody-wins situation. The telephone company, gas company, taxi cab associations, and several other regulated industries sued us and won. You are NOT free NOT to make a profit in Connecticut. Why, if you did, then how many others might choose social goals over private goals? Before this experience, I still believed it was a free country. Now I think of myself as living in a country that has falsely understood freedom.

There was an echo in this experience that was quite strong. I was not free not to make a profit. I was not even free to model forms other than private ownership. Goliath had turf to protect against David's stones.

The echo was my own internal battle with upward mobility. I never felt free not to succeed in social terms. Parents, campus ministers, teachers, and friends would have withdrawn respect. My track record would suffer. Their respect proved to be a form of control; it was their own notion of morality that they were protecting and that was worth the price of controlling me, someone they actually loved to the best of their abilities.

When individualism protects the private morality as thoroughly as it does, things get more and more out of whack. Schools don't teach, doctors don't heal, jails don't rehabilitate, and then welfare reproduces itself. We see the syndrome most noticeably in the way we "help" the poor. Two out of every three welfare dollars leave the south side of Chicago on the train every night in the pockets of a social service professional heading home to the suburbs.

When care becomes a function of a system, which communities do not control or which they have abandoned, it is not care. It is a commodity, something that is bought and sold, and that is why it feels like one. No one can be paid to do what communities have forsaken.

To understand the hold that such large systems have on us, we have to look no further than our own language. The coded language of the human service economy has entered the vocabulary of the street. Anguish becomes mental illness. If stuck in a traffic jam, we can easily hear a commercial on our car radio advising us to use product X to MANAGE our pain or to BUY a health club membership so we can relax. We are lifted above the traffic jam by a barrage of advertising, the code of which is to buy and consume an ever-changing personal image. No one suggests the cause of traffic as too many cars. The addictions that these advertisements develop are immense: We dare not be satisfied, and few are. We dare not be stable. "Moving up," as the Mayflower moving van ad puts it, condemns us to cycle from a small apartment to a larger one and on to a mansion. Mayflower needs our business and knows how to get us to give it.

This labeling of our middle class experience as "moving up," and managing the pain along the way, is demonic. The labeling of the poor as "needy" is its twin. In the same way that we are not free not to make a profit, we are not free to not move up. If poor, we are not free not to be needy. The labels become our language, advertising the dominant form that speech takes.

Communities have forsaken their streets and forgotten their language. The morality that prescribes this loss is that of privatization. It is individualism unhinged and out of control. Communities have the capacities to restore their streets but not without a serious bout with the morality now systematized into a powerful political, economic, and linguistic knot.

We dare not indulge the illusion that understanding this knot and the hold it has on us will give us the power to change things. To be morally restorative without attending to the scale of the political economy that enshrines individualism is one of the worst offenses that is possible. The objective consequences of war, poverty, race, gender, environmental pollution and exhaustion, technological capacities not servant to human purposes, and the like will continue to require our best strategies of advocacy, organization, and development. We will have to be political in ways none of us have yet considered. So slick is the system's morality and so slippery our foot in a new public vision that we will find ourselves playing the private individual games we know so well in almost every endeavor. Lots of people feel that they have given their best to public initiatives and that these initiatives just don't work. What they mean is that they got hurt in a community organization or a development project or a congregation. They came together with other people, had their hopes raised, felt empowered, and then difficulties in the community itself intervened. Somebody's ego got out of control. Somebody stole money. Somebody treated someone else cruelly. The meaning of these disappointments is not that politics don't work. The meaning is that we don't know how to work communities. We have been too well trained in the old system to know how to behave collectively. When we understand these failures in our own development as people, we will be ready for the political challenges that lie ahead.

Religious communities bear a particular responsibility and carry a special gift in the creation of counter cultures. We have a tradition that eloquently lays the problems of war and poverty, race and gender in covenant denial, in hardness of heart, refusal of the gifts of creation. We are the original environmentalists in our complex storied place in the land. We are not unfamiliar with sin and have no reason to reduce it to privacy or individual error — or, finally, to fear it. The effectiveness of total culture can be seen most brilliantly in its capacity to trick biblical people into confusing sin with impoliteness or drinking or swearing. In this privatization of sin, and its confusion with forgiveness then as personal salvation, people confess to the wrong things. People come to church for all the wrong reasons.

Alcoholics Anonymous is probably a better example of church than most of what goes on Sunday mornings across the land. In AA, we have confessed sinners, gathering without professional leadership, desperately aware of their need for one another and for community, radically committed to God, and aware that their liberation and therefore their life depends on their ability to depend on each other rather than alcohol. Sunday mornings at eleven a.m. enjoy none of these religious requirements. Instead we have people looking for individual relief from individual wrongdoing. Since only the truly stupid dare think they are responsible for the trouble that blights their experience, the confessions are phony. And so is the absolution. We know deep down that war is not our sin alone, that poverty is not only ours. We may tag along with the privatized morality, but we don't actually believe its systematized truth.

If there is one thing that congregations could do to break out of their hypocrisies into community, that one thing would be to cease the professional practice of referral. People do knock on church doors all the time, but too often we send them empty away. We refuse them because we think we have nothing to offer. In fact our communities are the very thing that people need. In our blindness to the very gifts we contain, we make lethal mistakes. When we refer, we refuse the stranger and hand him or her back to the culture. Rather than acting on our knowledge of the healing capacities of communities over experts, we act on the falsehood of professionalized care. We even refer our own when they become too complex or strange. Seminaries train pastors in referral through the dominance of clinical models; lay people are quite convinced of the impropriety of their care in marital difficulties, or teenage suicide, or drug addiction. Most will back off if asked to call on a troubled family in any of these situations on the grounds that "they wouldn't know what to say."

Here we see the reinforcing cycle that disempowers communities. Like an unused muscle, communities that refuse to care for their own and the stranger become flaccid. We are reduced to poignant prayers at the concerns time in the service and to passivity growing among us.

Recently I had a chance to observe what happened to a woman who came to a poor church for help. She was putting booze in her baby's bottle every night so he would go to sleep, so she could go to sleep in order to get up to work in the morning to pay for his uninsured birth by C-section. She came to tell someone the story. Her life did not allow much time for friends. At the church, she was sent to a caseworker at the Department of Children and Family Services. Had she been brought into the community, she might have been helped and forgiven. She might have stayed on to help others. She might have found a friend. In the right community she could have been helped to understand the anger she had at the black teenager who had been next to her in the hospital and was delivering her third child at the state's expense. Here we have a fee for service medical system joining with racism and sexism to box a woman and her child. She needs help with her racism if it's not to grow. Where exactly is the child's father? These concerns belong to communities to unravel. They make us strong as we engage them and weak as we deny them.

Before that, I had been shocked by a very different kind of church doing fundamentally the same thing. A United Church of Christ minister from another part of the country called to get help for his daughter who was being beaten by the man she lived with. I was the only UCC minister who lived in that town whom he knew. And me, he knew only slightly. I got in touch with the UCC church in the neighborhood of the man's daughter, and they referred her to the battered women's shelter. I was furious. Why could they not have found a home for her? The congregation had over a thousand members. Her father was right; she was ready to make her move out of the place where she was being beaten. Now I have to wonder who I can call if someday my daughter, God forbid, is in trouble far away. I assume I am part of an extended family in the UCC. There's nothing wrong with battered women's shelters, but this woman didn't need one. She is now staying with a member of another congregation who had been through a similar experience.

Both of these women's lives now have a much better chance of being enriched. So does the congregation that resisted referral.

In one case we refused one of our own. In the other we refused the stranger. In both cases it was the communities who lost, even more than the individual. They had a chance to grow in caring and they gave it away.

These tricks that big systems use to keep communities powerless are easily exposed. Because they parade under the banner of individualism as morality, people think they are doing the right thing taking care of themselves. Taking care of number one is so familiar that it sounds right. But only a quick glance at the demonic consequences of such privatism shows how wrong we can be just when we think we are doing right. Most congregations actually think they are doing right when they refer people to better services or more well-trained counselors. Most husbands actually think they are doing right when they tolerate a miserable boss for the sake of their family's financial future. Most women actually think they are doing right when they take pressure-filled jobs that prevent either themselves or their families from being nurtured. They have joined the rest of the world in taking care of number one. Most parents resist taking care of someone else's child in addition to their own on a playlot. They resist a PTA statement on a common grievance against a school. We feel enormous obligations to our own children and very few toward those about to inherit the earth.

Right in the middle of all this devastation of communities there remain countercultures of some strength. Women's groups that have lasted twenty years, families who actually gather in reunions, neighborhoods that have resisted the commandments of real estate brokers to move when color moved in next door, gatherings of college friends that last over the years, all these manage to happen for the lucky in our culture. Some congregations manage to create free spaces for communities to develop. They become havens for the mobile and points of light in blighted districts. It never ceases to amaze me how many churches there are in ghettos. The grocery stores leave, the gas stations leave, the welfare offices move out, and up springs a storefront church that gathers from the very ashes the capacities of the community to take care of itself.

For those who see how the tricks against community work and want liberation from the box of individualism, the best place to start is in denial of upward mobility. Acting against the prevailing private morality will probably make that choice a necessity, given that people who don't march with this society are quickly punished, but there is a mighty difference between not wanting an upwardly mobile job and not having one. If you can't cut the mustard and move up, as your marching orders read since first grade, if not before, you might be hurt or defeated. You might become one of those customary passive-aggressive types who has lots of hostility floating around but can't dare direct it at the systems that caused the hurt in the first place. These losers and wimps and ne'er-do-wells oddly are the leaders of communities. They are often the people who, if able to transform their social defeat in the dominant culture into social victory in a counterculture, have the graces of community. They don't imagine themselves on the top of every heap. They don't need to be head of every class. They're not about to move to the newest version of the Sun Belt after six months of getting to know you. Giving up on upward mobility in favor of community life is a conversion. Almost no one does it completely or well. This society prepares us too poorly for grace at community. But more and more people are listening to what their eyes and ears tell them about individualism and how much it hurts. We are choosing the imperfections of community over the enforced perfections of ladder climbing. Our blood pressure is lower. We are having a good time.

If the middle class restores community by jumping off the fast track, the poor find their way in affirmation of their own competence. Many systems feed off the neediness of the poor. As long as we have the poor, there is always someone who we can be better than. There is always a bottom to the heap. The poor are frequently much more knowledgeable about communities and their capacities for good and bad. When the poor realize this expertise, and deny the press releases about how pathetic they supposedly are, upward mobility and individualism will suffer. Unfortunately, too many poor people are just looking for their slice. They have joined the rat race in their minds, if not their behaviors, and joined the totalism of too many Americans looking for the same stupid thing, the same leg up on their neighbor or friend or relative.

It is important as we argue the restoration of community that we not idolize it. Like any good, community contains its own shadow. Even when the stranger is brought into the community, and there invited to make a home with others, even when we resist advocating for her or serving him, even then communities know how to stumble. It is very important to keep our technical mind off communities. Some set their jaws against individual differences altogether and thereby turn themselves grey. Their very art is failure not function. They are not and never will be perfect. The story of communities is one of never quite being all they could be while at the same time retaining hope in themselves and each other. Restoration by forgiveness is their movement. In communities, we are not trying to fix things. Instead, we are being. We are at home.

Oddly, this very reversal, the priority on being rather than becoming, allows for good work. Only communities can shut poverty off at its tap in greed. Only communities can stop war. Only communities can restore streets to dwell in and land to grow in and schools to learn in. They can do these things because they understand what's really important, which is their life together.

The streets will be restored when communities take back the powers they have given away. On that day the big systems won't have a prayer, and the communities will not need so many.

9
the
macy's parade
CHILDREN

the
macy's parade
CHILDREN

E VER SINCE I gave birth to three children, I have been the victim of a non-stop internal conversation. Donna Reed is talking calmly to an agitated former hippie. The ex-hippie says, ''Family life is a blast. So, lean back, relax, everything will be groovy.'' Donna Reed recommends planning, dour attentiveness, careful screening of all emotions. Donna and the hippie quarrel. They carry on.

The children, however, require decisions, not conversations. Thus, action wins the race against theory. I can usually only find out what I think by looking at what I've done. Thus I have had to find out what kind of parent I am by looking back at what kind of parent I have been. Neither Donna Reed nor the hippie has as much power as the deeds.

This mixture in me of Donna and the hippie is what ends up deciding what to do for fun, what to do for school, what to do for work. The big decisions of enchantments, competition, and the economy are all on my table every day, right along with my ghosts. First, to fun.

I can't really blame Macy's. It is hardly their fault that the parade enchants me so much that I began planning for this year's event last year at this time. My friends from Pennsylvania would take a hotel room in the city on their way to Riverhead. Their two teenage boys would give me the security I'd need to risk my three children under five to the crowded streets of Manhattan Thanksgiving Day. We'd take the train in early Thursday morning and be the first people at the head of the parade. Our view would be superb; our outsmarting the crowds a sign of our peculiar intelligences. The children would be putty in my powerful parenting hands. They would be happy. They would not complain. Like the vaulting balloons, they would float down Broadway on the crisp November air, remembering for all time the sugarplum specialness of Thanksgiving morning. No TV parades for my cherubs, only the real thing and that perfectly viewed.

The parade started on time even if we didn't. The children demanded breakfast on the way and had what less hearty spirits would call a quarrel in the deli over the nutritional difference between a chocolate donut and a plain bagel. The bottle of juice we bought had floating objects in it and had to be returned on principle. My friends did take the hotel room, and it was a very nice hotel room. We got there about 8:45 a.m., ready and raring, only to discover the two boys slouched under pilings of bedding in a way that only teenagers can. The parents were undergarbed for the parade. You can't wear pajamas to the Macy's Thanksgiving Day parade. This more mature family proceeded to read the paper, order coffee, and lounge about while my less mature children turned on the television and began to enjoy the parade. The least mature person in the setting, me, began to rush everyone. I used the children's short attention span as my excuse. It's a good thing these are old friends.

About 10:15, our party of eight (minus the two men who had taken the train back to Riverhead, mumbling insults about the myths of women and family holidays and how glad they were to be free of the entire operation) departed the hotel. We walked briskly across 56th Street, or at least as briskly as you can carrying three children accompanied by two sightseeing teenagers, whose interest in urban architecture seemed to spring full force out of the need to get to the parade. Photos of various cathedrals and the lobby of the Waldorf later, we arrived at the parade. Rather we arrived at the crowd that preceded the parade. I didn't have the courage to look at my watch. By now I was in a mantra mode: ''Relax,'' it said, over and over again, more loudly each diversion.

Thank God the Pink Panther was waltzing down Broadway just as we hit an opening. Before that, the kids were convinced that I had made the whole thing up. There was no Big Mickey. There was no music. There was no dancing in the streets, only walking, hungry walking, with nothing but knees to look at. Mommy has been telling us all these happy things for the last year, with a real speed-up in the last week, only for torment. Only to assure us that life might be enchanting if you were the kind of people who could get places.

We're not the kind of people who can get places. We are the kind of people who get delayed. Delis, friends, pretty steeples along the way.

For about fifteen minutes we watched the parade. That is, fifteen minutes minus the ten we spent in the bathroom. We got a great spot just off Times Square, and the kids only cried a little when the Pink Panther hit the Times Square digital clock. One, at the first sight of a cotton candy cart, remembered the chocolate donut he had been denied at breakfast and renewed that grief. Right about then Katie said she had to go to the bathroom.

I assumed my life was over. There were plenty of little joints interspersed between the kiddie porn outlets up the street on Times Square. I decided to take my chances on the holiday spirits of the fine citizens of New York. Thus we marched into a Chinese establishment of serious food-like smells looking as much like customers as we could. I really didn't want to buy a fried rice but figured I would if I had to. The restaurant was right next door to a movie "theater" that talked about things that little girls do in the night. As the hostess pushed a button and motioned to us to go down the stairs, opening the door while the loud button blared, I finally figured out one way that people were recruited for such movies and nearly panicked. I asked Katie if she really had to go, and she said "Yes." And so, hand in hand, we slid down those greasy stairs, forgetting for a moment how much enchantment we were missing. All plans were reduced to getting back up the stairs. When we used the bathroom, a wall on the stall fell down and missed Katie's head by inches. It had been attached by wires. Mantra kept playing, "Relax," only now it was playing more loudly.

We got back upstairs. We returned to the parade. The rest of New York had found our good spot. The Big Mickey had just been by. Katie said, "Don't worry, it will come back." I said, "Sure, next year." Jacob took my cynicism as an opportunity to repeat his claim about a chocolate donut, and that's why the two teenagers went off looking for one right at the end of the parade. I had lost my will. The fight was gone. A cop came up and asked us to move since Santa was coming down the street. Realizing that the parade was over, and that the Pink Panther was going to have to suffice as evidence for enchantment, broke that little piece of my adult heart that I reserve for such disappointments. We realized that we had a modest situation.

Splitting up right as the parade ended was like throwing your two needles into a haystack because you had two or three days to look for them. Jacob was inconsolable about the donut; Katie, about missing Big Mickey. It should be pointed out that what with all the noise, and the grease, and the smell, and Mom's anxiety attack in the bathroom that Katie really didn't have to go after all. That we were saving for now.

The boys came back fairly quickly with the donuts, no more than two or three years I'd say. They were out of chocolate. That did it. The sun had gone behind the buildings, and it was cold. Two children had to go to the bathroom. The cop kept saying things like, "Move along," and I tried to tell her that we really didn't know how to. The eighteen year old figured out how to trade Jacob one with chocolate sprinkles for the one with white frosting he was trying to pass off on him, and Jacob held that donut all the way through Thanksgiving dinner. He never ate it, he just held it. It was the most disgusting mass of sugar and flour I have ever seen. And I saw a lot of it, carrying it and Jacob all the way across Manhattan to the East Side, giving thanks that I had good enough friends to carry the other two that distance since Jacob's violation of the no carrying rule was so public. Imagine these same friends eating turkey with me (much) later in the day, donut, kids and all.

Now here's the unplanned thing. At the Waldorf Astoria we collapsed. We couldn't go another step against the crowd with thirty-five plus extra pounds in tow. Not to mention the healthy snacks we were still carrying. We had just toured the lobby on our way over, and no cops had thrown us out then. So in we went like we owned the place. We sat down on one of the brocaded chairs. The children stopped crying, decided that they weren't going to freeze to death, and that they might as well make the best of the situation. My friend went for the car. In the thirty minutes we waited, the children created games using the marble statues as toys.

Wolves, dogs, little Red Riding Hood, E.T., and the Pink Panther were all included. People stopped to observe the enchantment. All the animals were fed chocolate donuts. All the dangers were tamed. All the jackets were thrown on the floor. Only once, from behind a potted plant, where some so-called Indians were hiding, did a loud voice call out, "Who farted?", and thus only once did I see myself embarrassed by the splendor of the space challenged by the reality of my children. Otherwise splendor met splendor.

Unplanned enchantment may be the best kind. I don't know, I'm so busy, as I write, also planning for Christmas, hoping that this recipe or that toy or those candles will do the trick. The fun of preparation just can't be denied. I surely had more fun thinking about the Thanksgiving parade than I did while there. But for Christmas I am planning a little unplanning, just a little time to see accidental splendor and it to enjoy. My focus will be interesting delays — delis, friends, donuts, unusual steeples. There is just not enough time for everything to go well.

I should have learned this at vacation time when, instead of enjoying the vacation, my children enjoyed stopping more at the New Jersey Turnpike bathrooms and playing water games with the pink soap container and the funny turn-off-yourself faucet. For them, the destination was immaterial, the journey all. I should have learned this when Stripe, the caterpillar, found on one of the at least thirty-seven pit stops (times three) we made while driving through North Carolina, delighted the children for three hundred miles, causing them to set aside the strings and strings of Cheerios I had made for their entertainment. The number of ways my children have tried to educate me about arriving and its disappointments compared to the journeying — about the virtues of the special versus the ordinary and how you should never go out of your way for the former because the ordinary will carry within it all the special you need — the number of ways is astounding.

My son thinks that changing your favorite dessert from pumpkin pie to chocolate pudding is enough excitement for a year; I design excursions to the most exquisite pie shop on Long Island. He prefers the kind, "you know," that comes from the can. Why anything other than macaroni and cheese should be served for supper, or anything other than p and j's should be served for lunch, my children don't know. Why should I tell them? What good will it do for their palate to become as insatiable as mine? Certainly they will be better consumers, better travelers, better prepared for the fun of life. But on what basis would I rob them of simple satisfactions and exchange more sophisticated ones? Probably just to find companionship for my insatiabilities. Ordinary suppers will delight them at the same time that they are boring me.

Even our disasters fit this mold. I remember the time the twins were in their highchairs in our dining room in Chicago. There the walls were painted a lovely dusty rose. They were eating borscht, which was one of the oddball foods that they actually liked. It was that day that they discovered how to pong foods with a spoon, and they ponged a simultaneous, direct hit of borscht on the dining room wall. It wouldn't come off, and I considered the dining room permanently scarred. As we left that Chicago house, moving to New York, on my last walk through that empty but finally clean dining room, I noticed the borscht stains and burst into tears. I considered my grief for my children's fast-disappearing childhood inconsolable. All the time I had hated those stains on that wall, now they were becoming beloved memories, reminders of how much living went on in that less-than-perfect dining room.

Unplanning as a strategy would cultivate interruptions. It would cultivate an awareness of surprise, a capacity to count on surprise getting you through the narrow places where tight planning has put you. Unplanning would take a trip counting on caterpillars to show up. Think of all the bags we wouldn't have to carry. I can make a good case for it, my children can make an even better case, but I doubt that the wisdom will ever seep into the pages of my calendars or the length of my lists. Here I follow the orders of the advertisers and reach for all the gusto I can get. I train my children to do the same. I respond to ads about the simple life and then add to my list the procurement of the product that will provide it. No matter how knowledgeable I become about the folly of effort, the futility of efficiency, the political incorrectness of my lengthy lists and aspirations, nothing changes. Let time open up a little bit, let there be space with no plan in it, and I use the opening to refine my goals and increase my expectations. The children are figuring this out, and their greed is probably my strongest complaint against them.

They have discovered that the fundamental principle of my world is scarcity. Not enough. No category of enough. Never enough. Insatiability. As yet, they do not know how well this principle serves the culture that made it, and therefore me. They do not know upward mobility despite my efforts to teach it to them. They do not know that more is better, but quickly they are learning. "Jacob has three Reese's Pieces, and I have only two." Where do those kinds of statements come from? Mommy saying that we are wasting time standing in the parking lot counting the cars and demanding that we get in the car immediately. That's where. There is no point in naiveté. "We need more time," is Mom's major message. More time is better than now time. Little pitchers have big ears. Hippies have extravagant needs for enchantments; Donna Reed has equally strong desires for orderly fun. Both pressure the Mom who has little time for either.

Besides the way I persecute my children with enchantments I think I would have enjoyed, my problem as a parent is a lot my culture's problem with parenting. Not that I don't have wickedness of my own. I do. But mostly I err by incarnating the scarcity culture has taught me or by competing with the others crowded on this planet with me. That competition came with either my mother's milk or the public school system or both. It's been there so long that I really don't know what I would do without it. How would I know who I am without comparisons to others? How could I face the world without a bit of an edge, a smirk that says that I am at least as good as that drivel? Sometimes from this very perspective I think I understand why televised mediocrity is so comforting. At least I am better than that. To not compare would force me into a wilderness of values so serious that we'd probably never even find the car, much less get into it.

Probably that's why I made such a fool of myself on my son's first day of kindergarten. The public school system also made a fool of itself. I'd like to be able to say that I resisted, but I didn't. I made a pact with comparison and competition that day, a pact of which Mephistopheles would be proud.

Isaac had to be tested the summer before entering kindergarten. A few days before we got there for the test, his attractive, intelligent best friend, a girl, took her test. Her father (no hero in this little drama either) dropped to my husband that Sally had done extremely well on the test. In fact, said he, she was reading at the third grade level. I remember the precise twist that my intestine took at that news. Before we even got there, the web of competition was at work. I wanted Isaac to be reading at the third grade level. I did not want him not to be reading at that level. Reasonable? No. Attractive? No. Only factual.

We arrived at the school. I am a big enough fake that I am saying all sorts of groovy things like I'm sure you'll do fine on the test. Don't worry, etc. Imagine a mother with third grade blazing in scarlet on her chest telling a five year old to relax. Imagine a mother whose head is full of voices, hippie voices and Donna Reed voices, assuring a child there is nothing to worry about at big boy school. The hypocrisies are astounding, considering just how much there is to worry about at big boy school, and they did not fool the five year old for one minute. He took the test. He got every question right but one. The question he got wrong was about eyebrows, and by the time we got to that part of his drawing he was so bored that he was reading the alphabet over the blackboard. (Don't worry. I now make sure that my three-year-old twins each put eyebrows on their figures.) The guidance counselor congratulated him on taking a very good test and told me that he was quite advanced and would surely do fine in kindergarten. She was smiling. I was waiting for word on his reading level. When it didn't come, I said, "What is his reading level?" She didn't understand my question. She said, "We don't do that sort of comparison at this level." I said, "Oh, yes, you do. My friend so and so told me that his daughter was reading at the third grade level.'' She was amazed and said, ''No, I don't think we said that.'' Which maybe they did and maybe they didn't. Anyway, she asked me the tempting question of whether I would like to see Sally's test and compare it to Isaac's and I said, horrifying myself, ''Yes.'' I could have said no. I should have said no. She shouldn't have offered to show it, but she was trying to convince me that they didn't do those kinds of comparisons. Her evidence was that we do other kinds of comparisons, and thus she proceeded to show Sally's drawings and compare Isaac's drawings to them, with me eagerly analyzing along with her. Sally understood eyebrows. Finally I'd seen enough, both of eyebrows and my own insides, and I got her to put the file away.

It took me several days to tell even my husband that I had done this thing. I actually try very hard to keep my competition a secret. Confidential, as it were.

Tracking. SAT scores. Report cards. Valedictorians. National Honor Societies. These are some of the blocks I've lived on. Sometimes the living has been good, challenging me out of my slouch into something like quality. Keeping up with the Joneses takes some effort, and the results are knowing more about eyebrows rather than less. The results are skills, breadth, great capacity for criticism, the ability to tell the difference between the good and the really good. Competition has not been all injury to me nor will it be to my children. There is just too much of the world flowing in that direction. To refuse to compete is to counter culture in a way that it really doesn't understand. This culture is so good at getting inside us that most people, in countering culture, end up doing so competitively. We become more right than culture, more wise than culture, holier than culture. I learned this counter-culture trick well before I became an ex-hippie.

But there is also injury in competition, and a good parent would want to know its name before teaching her children too much compliance. The name of the injury, I think, is loneliness. It is standing so much on your own two feet and on the treasure of your own talents that you become blind to what communities offer and can do only together. Everything becomes something you have to do, something you have to dredge up out of your own aching intestines. There are no partners in the competitive world, only obstacles, only strengths that, instead of making happy, cause jealousy. If we want our children to be perpetually arguing over who has the most Reese's Pieces, competition will be a good thing to teach them. If we want a child who can be happy at the goodies another child has, competition will have to be fought. We certainly can't ignore it. It is too pervasive. But we can fight it, particularly if we let our children know it is our fight and not theirs. Someday I'm going to have to tell Isaac the story of his first day of school, and how Mommy messed it up by being more concerned about Sally and her potential to be Isaac's enemy than Isaac and his potential to have Sally as a friend. I'll also have to tell Sally's parents, my friends, about what I did, and, together, we'll have to decide if competition is our legacy for these children. By the way, Sally's mother is a very good writer. Why should the plot not thicken?

My friends and I will either raise our children to be as competitive as we are, or we will enter the wilderness of values, the place where we go once we have decided against competition and in favor of something different, something we know nothing about, something our parents didn't tell us. Raising children has a lot to do with things our parents didn't tell us. Raising children has a lot to do with things Donna Reed didn't tell us either. No wonder it feels so frequently like a long, interrupted meander through a giant parking lot, full of cars that look a lot like yours, with only a few people who remembered to attach something inspiring to their antennas so they could find their way back home.

I used to think that all the big issues in the parenting maze were summarized by the voice I kept hearing in my head, the Donna Reed voice. I even called it the Donna Reed problem with sarcasm in the days when the hippie voice was dominant. The problem is the assumption of harmony at home, the happy family in which all flourish and all nourish. Fifties' television seemed to enjoy the image so much that baby boomers are quite cursed by it. If we could just recognize conflict, thought I, and assume that all families had a lot of it, then we would navigate the rough waters more easily. But now I have been forced to complicate that simplicity.

Conflict is a much better theory for family life than harmony, to be sure. But the sources of the conflict require exposure. We have to be less confidential about what is hurting our families and more willing to tell the story of our trouble. Gender is a difficulty for families, and it is not our fault. Child care is a difficulty for families, and it is not our fault. Two incomes are a tremendous difficulty for families, and that pattern is not our fault. The absence of satisfaction that most adults have in their work is a difficulty for families, and it, too, is not our fault.

These systemic issues heighten the conflicts in families who would be well or healthy. It's not just that our parents didn't teach us good routes in the maze: They didn't know the routes. If anything, they were able to live more harmoniously in a hurtful culture because exposure was limited. There was plenty of incest in the old days, plenty of "wife-beating," plenty of family violence, but television didn't tell everybody about it all the time. You would not believe the number of women in their seventies and eighties who tell women pastors about what their fathers did to them. There was a blanket of silence. Now that some of these conflicts are out of the closet, many search for the roots of family disharmony. Many people wonder what it is that is making intimate life so difficult, and even more blame the difficulty on themselves. It must be me or him or her — we're the bad ones because we have trouble in our family.

As I have gone after the Donna Reed problem both in my own family and in those in my parishes, I have been forced to locate the source of family disharmony in culture as much as individuals. In women who hate being women because women are so undervalued economically. These women take out their anger on their husbands and children. In standards of living that have now ordered every adult out of the home for eight or more hours. Households weren't meant to exist without wives. Someone should be keeping the home fires burning or at least picking up the dry cleaning. This is an honored role, a central role, a happy place to work, but the role of housewife has been degraded: first, by the economic system that sent us all to work and then by feminists in a mistaken shot at it. We see no redemption of the role, only defensive actresses, telling us, "I'm just a housewife."

Imagine if you will, for one minute, a world where men and women worked four hours a day at a job and the rest of the time shared the jobs of keeping the house warm, putting wood on the fire of children's turbulence and each other's intensities. Imagine how much more interesting and less frustrated family disharmonies would become. Probably the most threatening thing to the planet right now is this absence of anyone centrally occupying the place of nourishment. It's so clear that the problem is social, economic, and political — and yet that clarity hasn't stopped one victim, one underfed adult, from blaming themselves for problems with their children or each other. Big systems love blame, especially when no finger is pointed at them.

On a less radical level, surely child care has to be counted as one of the systemic idiocies that require families to maintain dishar- mony. Of course if everyone didn't have to bow at the altar of the 9-to-5 day, we wouldn't need so much child care. As it is, we are desperate for good child care. But not desperate enough to pay people a decent wage for it. Eventually integrity requires us to stop wringing our hands about "our children" and what's to become of them. As long as check-out clerks get more money to put our food in our grocery baskets than child care workers do to nourish our children, we have no right to complain about what is happen- ing or not happening to our families.

Only the blind fail to see that the root of our family problems are economic. If you want to call me a Marxist, then go ahead. That will only get you a mysterious label to use against the reality of what I am saying. We think we have to work to take care of our families, and we think both parents have to work, and we think we should try to get as good a deal as possible on child care. These are economic decisions. We make them under compulsion of a culture that says this is what we must do. There really are no alternatives. And so we obey. But as we obey — and by the way, I do obey — we know that the set-up is wrong. That children are not getting the care or attention they need either from us or their workers. It is no mystery to us — really — why our children are competitive or greedy or undernourished emotionally. They are just like us because we haven't found another culture in which to raise them.

It's a lot like driving a car. A lot of people, and not just former hippies, don't really want to drive a car. We don't want to use up all the oil or cause a world war fighting over what's left. We don't want holes in the ozone layer or stinking air to breathe. But we drive a car because everyone else does, and everyone else drives a car because we do, and the cycle causes the economy of roads and oil and steel and cars to flourish. It flourishes; we flounder. We are back in our enormous parking lot and the shopping center wandering, while the kids are interrupting us about the overall scarcity of Reese's Pieces or some other fool thing.

Nobody can build a culture by themselves. Not one of us. Just because we attach a plastic rose to our antenna in the lot and therefore get our car quickly and get back home before the rest of the wanderers doesn't mean that we are any closer to reducing the conflicts in family living. No matter how pure or fast we become as individuals, culture will not be built.

Culture will have to be built on economic decisions. Families who choose each other over upward mobility. Who manage being poorer than the rest of the world, with grace. Who go much slower. The first group of people who refuse automobiles will go ridiculously slower than the rest of us.

My one clue to where to start in the parenting maze is in these economic decisions. How to work. What to work at. How much time to give to work. How and who to care for children with you. My fear is that most of us are so beaten down by the silliness of what we do all day long, by the absence of control we have — and think we have — over what we do all day, that we refuse to even consider these upstream questions. We content ourselves by walking

through large parking lots after hours knowing we are lost and competitively assuming that the rest of them are too. That is clearly one
competition that is winnable. We are all very lost. Almost no one
has a good way out of the maze of raising children and having families. The big systems have a genuine victory in this corner. Imagine
them having a genuine victory right in the corner that we love the
most, that in which we sit with our own flesh and blood, making
pro-family noises and working anti-family jobs.

Adults who decide that they won't be bored or trivialized by
their own work, adults who require decent jobs, jobs that make
them feel proud and useful, are the first step out of the maze. At
least then we won't add our own unhappiness to the systemic
oppressions that our children have. It is our job to take care of our
happiness, not theirs. The children have enough trouble locating
sufficient enchantments in places that adults have not approved.
The children have their own peace with competition to make. They
have their own genders to understand, their rapidly turning over
child care workers to comprehend. They have their own work to
find, their own meaning, their own points of complicity with culture,
and their own points of resistance. Adults will have to find their
own ways through the mazes of living and hope that little pitchers
will continue to have big ears.

Many parents learn too late that they will have to live beside
their children, not through them or for them. The best thing we
can give our children is our own best struggle with the important
matters of living. They'll receive that, and only that, whether we
"give" it to them or not. Little pitchers do have big ears.

Whether children will have to take parents or parents, children
to the new land of a new culture, I don't know. Probably we will
stumble along together, two steps forward and one step back. This
much I know. Neither planning, nor efficiency, nor competition will
get us there. Neither Donna Reed's best organization nor the
hippie's most fervent disorganization will lead us. Instead, the new
land will surprise us in decisions we have already made, disappointments from which we can learn. It will come as small places, little

pieces, just when we're too tired to go another step. I do not think we will get there by car because cars assume that big systems will continue to have us obedient to individualism. Speed will give way to a crawl. Confidentially, just between you and me, I think we'll get there by going together.

10
deep in
the double bind

MEN

deep in
the double bind
MEN

$\mathbf{A}$NY WRITING THAT gives big systems as much credence as this one does needs to conclude with attention to the areas of life where big systems are only part of the problem. For women, those unsystematized areas are at least men and children, which are labeled institutionally as marriage and family. Even in a thoroughly just, thoroughly sane world, we would probably still have headaches, and we would probably still not get along with every man who walks into our life. There would be days when the very children we adore we would put up for sale. Marriage and family, society assures us, are great ideas. Everyone should participate joyfully in them. Then comes the day that we realize we have entered relationships, not institutions. We find ourselves surrounded by real live men and real live children. They are no more or less normal or sane than we ourselves.

Not that the problems we have with men are not also functions of big systems. The name of this one is sexism, and both men and women are forged by it to disrespect and violate each other. Men think of women as sick, bad, crazy, or stupid, in Anne Wilson Schaef's great litany. Women think of men as leaky faucets, places where we pour our love down a sink and can't seem to stop. Many of us think of men as though they were the dishes. We hate the whole process but can't do anything else until they are dealt with. Until we are attached to a man, we find ourselves incomplete, dwellers in an unkempt house, unprotected in a dangerous world. Lesbians obviously don't have this problem except to whatever extent sexism has schooled them as well. For heterosexual women, however, being manless is problematic, almost as problematic as having one around the house. Yes, Virginia, there is a double bind when it comes to men.

Women who do have men around the house can think of lots of reasons to want to be alone, and women who don't, fantasize the opposite. Here I examine both sides of this double bind, that which propels us away from the commitments of marriage first and then that which propels us toward it. I have no routes of escape and, in fact, think of the double bind as something as inevitable as a headache, considering who men and who women both are and are trained to be. Recognition of the double bind yields a little freedom from it, and that is all I have come to expect.

In a future, non-sexist world, new jokes about the magnificent difference will have to surface. For now we must find humor in the realities of this moment; they are sexist and they are human. They come both with the turf of relationships across the great divide of difference, AND they are the pay-off a sexist society deserves for structuring such stupidities into our understanding of gender. Never forget the great "both-and" of feminist theory that the personal is the political is the personal. Obviously, men benefit from these stupidities about who women are supposed to be, and women suffer. It will be to the wiggle room, the small place of pre-revolutionary freedom, that I will write here — not how to change or transform a sexist society, which we must and will do, but how to live, married, in one until the transformation is complete.

We have only to listen in on the great women of history to hear the double bind. Amelia Earhart wrote to her husband on the morning of their wedding, February 8, 1931, that she considered marriage an attractive cage.

Charlotte Perkins Gilman set out to prove that a woman could work and love too. Two marriages later she realized that her experiment was unfinished. As a theorist, driven to join marriage to love and wean it from necessity, to oppose the thwarting of women's energy in domestic chores, she tried very hard to forge a woman-based view of marriage. She failed. Her conclusion was that a woman's professional ambitions collided head-on with her intense desire for love.

Edith Wharton uses the obvious tension between love and self successfully in many of her novels. She is driven like the others to seek happiness in marriage despite the defeat that her divorce and tragic affair yield. Women continue to press for intimacy even knowing how awful it can be.

Vita Sackville-West managed her enormous appetite for intimacy by a conscious strategy of rejecting monogamy. It is hard to find a notable Western woman in the last two centuries who was not well-versed in that strategy for excitement. They may have sought happiness in marriage, but most also had the sense to look elsewhere as well.

I have often mused on the fact that many women write while on the move, between things, in non-domestic spaces. Edith Wharton completed *The Reef* as soon as her divorce was over. Henry James commented then on how strange it was that a woman's creativity should erupt as a marriage fails and a household is dissolved. But it is not strange at all. Simone de Beauvoir did her best work in cafes. She neither made nor found a home in which to work. Margaret Mead's three marriages were all punctuated by travel. On the move away from home, she found the freedom to work. There is actually an odd pleasure women take in working outside the home, on the move, in the places where there are no dishes, no beds to make.

Sylvia Plath let the heroine of *The Bell Jar* describe household detail so vividly that the details themselves carry suicide notes.

Emma Goldman became a theoretician of the problem. She argued that marriage is an economic arrangement, an insurance policy. Emma Goldman also married three times.

In the world before birth control, women married more naturally, and some marriages were notable for the degree of emancipation and happiness enjoyed. One gets the sense that Elizabeth Cady Stanton actually loved her husband and was not at all overwrought to be called home because he was having a tooth extracted. On the other hand, there is no doubt that her daily round of chores and children in Seneca Falls depressed her frequently. There will always be exceptional unions.

The search for heroines who are happily married will be a long one. We can guarantee that if the women were unhappy and wrote about it, the men fared no better. The search will also persist for the women who, seeing and stating their evidence that marriage is problematic as a system, decided against it. Women can neither find happiness in traditional marriages nor stop looking for it there.

The complaints of notable women against marriage boil down to three. First, it is captivity, Earhart's attractive cage. Second, it prevents them from doing their work, Plath's bacon and eggs. Finally, it is boring, Sackville-West's monogamy. Outside of marriage woman after woman feels free, gets her work done, and finds excitement. Yet, these liberties do not satisfy and the urge to be caged, the urge to avoid the use of talent, and the urge for a legitimated regularity persist.

Women look for the solutions to these problems in all the wrong places. We assume that the right man will come along, one who will provide both boundary and liberty, encouragement in work and the same in intimacy, excitement and security, longevity of relationship, and tolerance of changes. He will also help with the laundry. Just because Virginia knows the truth about Santa Claus does not mean that she will resist hanging her stockings up. We mightily prefer dreaming about the right man to thinking about how marriage systematizes trouble for women.

The psychological burdens are easier to bear than changing sexism and its droppings. We come to enjoy the jokes about how having a man around the house is almost as bad as not having one; the persistence of conflict between the sexes keeps George and Gracie in business, and keeps us all assured that we are on the right track with our men if we can't stand them. They come to feel the same way about us. This peace we make with the systemic roots of our sexual dissatisfactions is what throws the issue of men and women into the universal, non-systemic arena. There we dabble with the trouble, romanticizing our pain as purposeful, as inevitable, as all part of the game.

Because I have never known any female who got along with any male in anywhere near the degree of harmony that she gets along with other females, I have laid down my sword against this interpersonal sexism. I don't expect it to go away anymore. It seems that men and women are in fact different and that we will simply have to start there in talking about what we are supposed to do next.

Whether the sources are biological or not, I have no idea. That they lie beyond the normal organizational or political capacities to change them is what's clear. The anthropologists and other geniuses are going to have to locate the sources; I won't live or love long enough to deal with anything but the consequences.

You'll want evidence. I'll start with the way most women don't leave men who beat them. Consistently don't leave them, even when the financial issue is not key. I dare say men, as they are understood, would leave a woman who beat them with great ease. I'll point to my two boys and one girl. They have two working parents; both parents did their diapers and do the dishes and fold the laundry. Both parents leave for work in the morning. The children are quite vocal about who the better cook is, and it is not the female partner. They have not had anything near a traditional gender arrangement when it comes to work outside or inside the home; their nursery schools and day care centers have all been vanguard in the ''Free to Be You and Me'' record business. Yes, all their teachers have been female. Otherwise they have been protected from the overt sexism of the traditional arrangements in these matters.

Nonetheless, my two boys are very boyish, and my girl is very girlish. She is extremely concerned about relationships; they are extremely concerned with their prowess and their toys. The two boys fight and she intervenes. She hates pants and prefers dresses, the frillier the better. I could go on telling you the gender differences that have been hitting me over the head since these children were born. I can't look the other way anymore. There is something real and different in these children, and one boy and one girl are twins. They don't even have the biological excuse. If it were just that my children were showing me these patterns, I'd not even speak. But my friends are telling me the same things. My classes are showing me the same things. Granted, there are exceptions. Maybe one out of every ten girls, one out of every ten boys breaks the mold. I delight when I meet them. But they are not evidence against the mold. The mold is there.

My experience in marriage is that a man can try very hard to be a wife in a family, but that he will only be able to go so far. He will not emotionally administer a situation but rather attempt to solve it. (Administration can be done gracefully, openly, non-manipulatively.) He will not hold close to his breast the dust in the kitchen cabinets. He will not see that dust as an accusation, nor will he be embarrassed if his mother comes to call and it is still there. If she is offended by the lack of spotting on the children's laundry and therefore the dirt that stays on their clothes, he will not be bothered by his mother's offense. That shame will be born by the woman who should have done the spotting or, at least, to earn her gender stripes, worried about it not being done.

A man is very unlikely to plan family outings or "dates" or remember his in-laws' birthdays or the date Grandma died. He is very unlikely to respond obediently to the teacher's request for eight cookies with faces on them by tomorrow, or to take kindly to the fact that it is Mickey Mouse Day at nursery school and someone is going to have to show up with some Mickey Mouse stuff, even if that means standing in the line at the local discount dive. And even the best of men are bad at dry cleaning.

What working women need is a "supportive" husband, which euphemism means somebody to help with the homemaking. What those who are blessed with such husbands get are men who will do housework but rarely males capable of homemaking. The training just isn't there. The mind set isn't there. Again, all these comments are limited to my own experience. Things are changing every day in this arena, and soon there are sure to be men who can make homes out of houses. There were not any at all until just recently. And surely there were none when our historical panel was writing against marriage while remarrying.

My final piece of evidence that men and women are significantly different comes from the behavior of the historical panel. These women were accomplished, intelligent people. They married over and over again because that's what accomplished intelligent women do. We (and there are many of us) want a man around the house more than we want to be free of the difficulties of having one around the house. We really wouldn't know what to do with ourselves alone. Nobody has ever imagined a woman alone and what her life would look like. We tend to sympathize with those who ended up alone, as though they were partial or unfulfilled. The notion of old maid is nowhere near dead.

Most women really do want to be married. Despite what we

know of marriage as a cage, we still want it. We still hope that ours will be different, that we can have freedom and commitment, cake and icing, all enjoyed with no calories. You don't have to speed along with heterosexual women to know that most of what they talk about is men. He did this, he did that, he said this, he said that. In college and high school these conversations peak, but it's not strange to hear them at the health club, the woman's circle, the grocery store, the nursery pick-up. Many women are preoccupied with men.

We know the social penalties if we don't have one. Parties alone, odd glances, a certain paternalism. We know the economic penalties too. Our fifty-nine cents on the dollar just doesn't go as far. Even after married women have seen the slats of the cage, have experienced the boredom, have wasted their life down the nightly drain of dishes, even then many women consent to matrimony. The social and economic penalties are too strong not to.

We have grown up in a world where we were told our duty was to complete a man, that we were incomplete without one. It's such a lovely idea that we have all hung on to its hope, long after the hope's evidence is past.

Oddly, what most women really want is a little time alone. Just a little. Not a lot. Over and over again in the feminist literature and in conversations with friends, as well as in my own yearnings, I discover this need for a room of one's own. It is the most powerful yearning I know of in women. Most would cook the whole Thanksgiving meal and clean it up gladly if one hour of solitude preceded or concluded the big day. Just one hour like Tillie Olsen wanted "to sift." Oddly, what the woman who got this one hour would do would be to think about others, how the meal went, who wanted what next year, who said what to whom, which child seemed preoccupied, which child had a really good time, what her husband looked like at the end of the table, how Aunt So and So seemed really to be failing. Relationships don't disappear in solitude; they just take on a quieter, less threatening form. We are no longer afraid that we may be gobbled up in solitude. There we remember that we would like to offer a little more of ourselves to be consumed. There is a difference in giving yourself away to relationships and being demanded by them. A big difference. Only the margin of time that frames activity permits the giving to go on.

Because so few of us women structure solitude into our experience, it is tempting to blame sexism for all our troubles with men. (May Sarton, a writer whose work I adore, is constantly complaining about how she can never get any time alone. Come on, May. Just take it.) It is easy to set up our choices as being with men, or friends, or children, or family, or being alone, when actually our choices can include others as long as we take back some of ourselves from them. No economic or political revolution (which will be needed to stop sexism in its tracks) can solve this problem women have of being too much with others. We simply have to take some of ourselves back. We have to save some of ourselves for ourselves. On Thanksgiving Day we simply have to open the door and walk out of the house for our hour, or open the door to our room and lie down on our bed and read for an hour. We have to do what we say others won't let us do. We have to start thinking of ourselves not just as people who need an hour of peace, but as people who deserve an hour of peace. This revolution is a spiritual one. It involves our decisions, our self-controls, our thinking far enough through the double bind of love and work that we begin to understand what it is we need and stop assuming that Mr. Right or some economic or political revolution is going to give us what we need. We have to take what we need, and we may.

Of course there are tremendous time binds. Women love to do everything perfectly. To give everybody in the world all the time they need, while forgetting that we ourselves need some time if we are to be able to give time to others. The double bind of work and family is probably public enemy number one for women. Odd, isn't it, how fully we give ourselves to the experience of the double bind?

If work goes well, we feel guilty about not stoking the home fires. If marriage makes us feel as if we are in a maximum security prison, we bemoan our capacity for intimacy. If we become bored, we accuse ourselves of excessive intensity. If we achieve autonomy, we resent the loss of relationship. If we achieve relationship, we grieve for autonomy. If we get that blessed hour alone daily, we get paranoid. What am I missing? Who said what to whom while I was out? Can you imagine people carrying on relationships without us managing them?

The double bind would perhaps be less forceful if only famous or accomplished women had the tension. We could introduce a theory of exceptionalism, identify the price of greatness, and pay homage to the struggle that produces character. After all, famous men have similar tensions. Few ask that genius coexist with regularity. But the struggles of the notable tell only part of the story of intimacy exchanged for solitude or public work in the lives of women.

The astonishing growth in the poverty of single women with children in the last decade proves the economic arrangement theory once and for all. These women are caught between a rock and a hard place, living with a man to pay the rent or divorcing him for a little peace or quiet or safety. Couple after couple in my congregation walk in with similar complaints to the notable women. She wonders why she is grading papers and making a grocery list at the same time. She worries about home while at work; he does not, and she knows it. She worries about the quality of their relationship in a way that he does not. To her, it is a part of her identity; to him, it is simply part of a much larger whole. For her, it is a constant fruitless search to find what Tillie Olsen calls a "rhythm of my own," "a time to remember, to sift, to weigh, to estimate, to total." He doesn't understand why she can't relax.

When asked if she would marry again, a fifty-four-year-old divorced woman who raised four children alone while teaching says, "I used to think every night that I would and should remarry. But now I'd really rather not." Her learned experience crystallizes.

She has found a way to live with herself. If more women could make this choice after divorce, and make it happily, the double bind would relax its hold on us. We need to want men less. When we want them less, we may discover that we can tolerate them more.

If anything is to be done about the boredom of marriage, or its competition with work, or its captivity of our better selves, it is we who are going to have to do it. We will have to amuse ourselves inside or outside of marriage. We will have to get our work done and "steal" the time if necessary from relationships. We will have to walk out of the attractive cage. Certainly no one else is going to do that for us, not Mr. Right, not even a feminist revolution.

The experience of divorce is higher education at its best for women. There we must examine our experience, we must come to terms with the genuine, serious, real differences between men and women (these are not the biological ones but rather the social ones); there we must find out if we are worth anything on our own or not. When I divorced my first husband, someone very close to me said, "You are not worth anything without him." The person was wrong, but it took me a long time to understand how and why.

The fear that they were correct in their assessment of me was severe. Obviously, I had been better schooled as a girl and woman than I ever thought. It seemed believable to me that the state of unmarriage was a state of nothing. What turned out to be true was that the state of unmarriage, of being single and adult, was marvelous, liberating, fun — all the things that I had been taught to think of as undesirable for a woman. God knows what women will do with freedom if we get it. Well, all I did was to have a really good time and then remarry, settle down, and have children. The only moment I really felt like a nothing was when someone dear to me said I was one. Sexism works this way: We believe what everyone else tells us about us. When we stop believing, we'll be on our way to turning sexism on its ear.

We might even walk straight into the hope of the double bind, that side of genuine interest in men and having them around. Instead of using them to complete ourselves, we might discover that there are parts of their difference from us that we genuinely like. The warmth of their embrace. Their arms. The wonder of the sexual approach. The wisdom in their spin on reality, the very reasonableness of it, if shed of the privilege. Their hands. The combination of strength and vulnerability.

The awesomeness of the hurts they have received at the hand of masculinity. Their skills with screwdrivers. The joys a father takes in a son or daughter. The manic ways they have of being nervous. Their courage. The way they walk the same planet as we do.

There is a cabin on Cape Cod that sits about a quarter of a mile back in the woods from the bay. It has weathered shingles, two rooms, loads and loads of healthy red geraniums flower-boxed on the outside. The outdoor shower is secluded, as is the small table in the back yard. I am pretty sure the cabin was made for me and me alone. I, in some part of my heavily related life, am meant to live there. To live alone and every morning to have for breakfast just what I want to have, to clean up my mess in less than two minutes, and to not even worry about lunch or dinner until my walk is over and the writing begun. Here I do not have to dress three children for school. There is not a lunch box in sight. My husband's magazines and papers are for once and for all disappeared. They are not on my counter, under my bed, in my bathroom, or stuffing the mailbox. The only papers anywhere in sight are mine. Likewise the magazines. If I am sitting on the couch with a blanket over my legs, reading the Psalms, slowly, and just get to a good part that I want to digest, no one, absolutely no one, comes in asking where his shoes went. The quiet is deafening.

In fact, the quiet is so deafening that I probably call Warren up on the third night and ask if he can come over. He arrives in a swirl of activity. I'm pretty sure when he comes he arrives with bags and bags of groceries because he will be appalled at how clean and sparse my food cabinets are. No doubt he will bring the *Village Voice* and a few other depressing left-wing journals that I really should look at. He will not want my memory to go bad, he will not want me to forget the latest evildoings in Ethiopia. We will have drinks. We will eat abundantly. We will talk as though talk had just been invented. We will make love. In the morning I will remember that he doesn't talk at breakfast and have an overwhelming desire to clean up the place, to re-sparse it, to repossess it. I will want him to go home. I will want to be alone but will probably ask him to come back the next night. I'd prefer to talk to him every day but just on the phone. The more alone I am, the more things of interest I have to tell him. That's my bind, double and all.

I meet lots of people who feel this way, whose urgency for their own space collides head on with their urgency for male companionship. No one is really looking for Mr. Right, just Mr. Not So Bad. It took me a lot of looking to find Warren; even him, I'd like to get away from, from time to time. That bumper sticker about how many frogs you have to kiss before you find Prince Charming is so true, it is almost unspeakable. Women who are dating have my deepest sympathy. Men are a tired lot, a silly lot, so many of them having closed their eyes entirely to the veritable renaissance in women that is going on right now on our shared planet.

Women are forming relationships with each other that are deeply sustaining. Sexual relationships between women seem like a good idea to many, so rich are they in guarantees that we will get along and be able to talk to our partner. Many women are choosing, even if not conjugally, to live together and to pay the rent by cooperating on it. The deep and abiding conversation that marriage can be need not be restricted to women and men, it seems to me. There are plenty of ways to find intimacy, and women should not wait for men to join us in the renaissance of intimacy now so full and available among us. Nor need women who are attached to men keep their attachment so traditionally. As married women, we need to find less oppressive ways to be married. We need to take the time for ourselves that we need. Our husbands are not chaining us to the couch or the armchair, and if they are, that's the best reason I can think of to march out of the house.

Between now and the time that sexism drops dead, women have a lot of chances for solitude, for freedom, for good conversation, even for marriage. We can spend all our time doing the dishes, or we can get beyond the cleanup. Even way down deep in the double bind there is a little wiggle room, a little place to call home, a little place to go when we need a room of our own. We may even invite a friend to join us in that room from time to time.

11
telling
the stories

BEGINNINGS

telling
the stories
BEGINNINGS

I WROTE THESE narratives to deepen my experience of social change. I wanted to find out if the powerlessness in and around me was real. Were women getting the often cited "nowhere" in the church? Was class actually such an underground subject as to make it unintelligible? What difference does it make to a person's politics as he or she ages or wearies? Is burnout something people inevitably experience at mid-life or is our generation uniquely drained? What meaning does violence or poverty have as they touch our lives? What are the spiritual powers that matter? What about church? Communities? Families?

I've been able here to tell a number of stories of how I've seen big systems affected by small people in small places. I don't think I've described progress because that assumes I think things were worse and are now improving. Actually I have more respect for the past than that and more hostility towards the present. Showing progress was less the purpose than showing hope, than demonstrating that what we do matters.

The big systems have so accentuated the large against the small, the many against the few, the much over the little, that they have practically convinced us that we are useless. And thus, under the cover of mass society, we all disappear into an ever-growing powerlessness. As though our smallness could never matter against its bigness.

As a frequent victim of the thoughts of these big systems, I have tried to fight these messages. They can be quite convincing in their assurance that we'll only experience a human world when we've become big and important and have a large audience. Oddly, what I have learned in these reflections is just the opposite. We will have no social change if the big and important are assigned to make it. It is precisely the big and important who have the most reason to oppose change. Should we ourselves actually achieve the power we so often say we need, we would become equally untrustworthy in the very process. The system elevates a few to its rewards on the top of the heap. Nobody on the top of the heap is motivated to jump down. Only those muddling around in what the system leads us to think of as the heap — which is actually our life in community — are likely to produce change in the ethos of the system. Only they who are small and insignificant (from the top view) can be trusted to turn the tables. Only those who have seriously given up power can dare to have it or to be trusted with it. If we change the system by its own manipulative methods, then there will be no change at all, just a rearrangement of the chairs on the same old Titanic.

I've tried to learn to sniff the systems' presence. Their themes are that "they" are big and we are small, they know and we don't, they are inevitable and we are accidents, they are normal, eternal, and natural, and God only knows what that makes us! They convince us that women can't get anywhere in the church. We are all class bound. Aging stinks. We're all about to burn out or already burnt out. The poor are poor and that's that. Violence is everywhere. Men are impossible; children are costly. You can't get good help, especially in a church where you dare not trust lay people with anything. There is enough negativism to go around. Whenever I pressed for solutions or ways to the other side of the complaints, I would be told about power. How we had to get a lot of power or at least get a hold of a local TV station or a million dollars.

I learned that you could almost always sniff out a system when people started to vociferously argue its inevitability. "Don't be silly," we'll hear. "You can't change that." "Darling, you can't even think differently about that." In some cases I've been asked not to even use the words. For example, *class* is not supposed to be said out loud. It makes the systems' defenders uncomfortable. A system can be sniffed out when the arguments turn to the *inevitable*, the *normal*, the *natural*, and people are yelling as they use these otherwise religious words. Granted, often the yelling is just designed to protect us, just designed to keep us from getting hurt, the way the yeller got hurt. But protection is rarely what adults are looking for when they hope. We don't need protection; we need partners. If we had a few partners, we wouldn't need protection at all.

I would hear these conversations at the tables of ordained women who were eating much better food than their parents. Far from burnout or rust, these speakers of despair were healthy, middle-aged, fairly free people. Activists, they had battled all the "isms." They really understood a lot about the world, including all the conflicts that living deeply makes apparent. But still there was a heaviness about my generation. I was conversant with it myself. It seemed to be something that we borrowed a voice to say, this despair, something that we almost parroted, as though we had been told to say it this way, given orders by our captain or something. The sound was tinny, full of obedience. The despair might have had a different tone if we were speaking with our own voice. Despair has just as much a possibility of being genuine as any other emotion. But this powerlessness was surplus, as Michael Lerner puts it. It was extra. It was over and above the genuine horrors we were facing. Yes, the racism, and violence, and sexism, and class divisions were and are real. But, as Thoreau advised the salmon on the fast developing Merrimack River, we had our fins against the tide. Rather than miring in the mud of the persistence of these systems — and they do persist, despite our best efforts — might we not be proud of the positions of our fins, might we not enjoy our community swimming upstream, might we not be glad that we were against the garbage and thereby enjoy each other and the swim?

Apparently the answer is no, not all the time. We need to repeat what the system has instructed us to repeat. Not until you are big will you matter. Not until you have power will value be yours. Georgia O'Keeffes matter; people who enjoy painting do not. We have been to school in this society's values, and we have learned well. What we have learned is despair and powerlessness at being small. It is society's way of telling us who's who and what's what.

Empowerment happens when the small stop taking orders and decide to have value as small, not to have value once big. To blow up the deflated places will require a reevaluation of small. Small will have to come into its own as small. If it gets big in that process,

I imagine we'll just have more enemies. If it can stay small, and local, and connected, I imagine we'll have more friends. What it will take to convince a million people to look at their life in this way, I don't know. That strikes me as a big system question. In small places we give our time to each other and see what happens.

My purpose in writing here has been to demonstrate the power of small places over big systems without being a jerk about it. I have actually been writing with some of my friends and congregants in mind, mostly friends I've known in various hand-wringing communities over the years. I've wanted to address the theme of helplessness as I've heard it expressed, and the only way I knew to do that was to tell stories. I think I'll stay in that mode and tell why a certain Episcopal clergywoman I met briefly at a meeting gave me a great deal of hope. I'm quite sure I'll never meet another one quite like her.

She was addressing a meeting of clergy and seminary professors gathered to discuss the future of theological education for urban ministry. The conversation had the tone I've described above: helpless, powerless, resigned, following orders to be so, no one risking their own voice, just the clack of parrots repeating what we thought we were supposed to say about our enemies' strength and our weakness. It was very dull.

In walked my hope wearing a Guatemalan blouse with clergy collar discreetly sewn in, a big smile on her face, and high heeled tennis shoes. She gave a presentation on one of the Pauline epistles, from the Greek, and exploded meaning all over the room. What the early Christians meant by conflict. What they meant about unity. How they thought. How distinct their world was from our world. How multi-faceted, how rich in valences almost unavailable to us over the centuries.

I'm always in a good mood when a woman excels in front of a mostly male crowd. It pushes my revenge buttons. But to see a woman do this while being sexual and funny at the same time was a total delight. Most of us make choices to chop off part of our identity to please the crowd we need to please. Certainly women clergy have become very dowdy while trafficking in the male world. The dowdiness is protective coloration, and, given all the sexual harassment we face and have faced, it's a decent strategy. But there is loss in disguises, and we have felt keenly those losses.

Thus to see someone make a different choice, make a choice not to hide parts of herself so that other people will feel more comfortable, is delightful. It is hopeful. She prayed that day that we "holy ones" would find our way. I think she meant ordained people, but, again, was using language that made people listen. It was not the captain's language. She was certainly not following instructions. She was thinking and speaking for herself, out of herself, out of her undisguised self. The high-heeled tennis shoes were a sign of the exuberance she knows because she spends so much time being herself, instead of following orders.

No, there are not five hundred Episcopal clergywomen just like her. There never will be. No, she is not gathering clones or disciples. Bigness is not her destination. If she is anything like other idiosyncratic souls I have known, she is probably seriously obnoxious in parts of her life. This very important fact about heroes and heroines can't be stated enough. Just because we all agree that someone is wonderful doesn't mean they should be our leader. It just means that a few parts of them are absolutely terrific. It takes communities to get places, each person rowing on their side of the boat at the right time. Big systems like to set up people as leaders so they can be knocked down when people realize their limitations. Small place people understand that even the best leader will not get us where we need to go. We'll have to make our own collective way, and nobody is going to get us off the hook of our own piece of the journey.

Thus, what is wonderful about my hope is that she is what she is, not that she is a sign that Episcopal clergywomen will be the leadership for a changed world. Big system thinking sets us up for making our good too good, so that we can revert as quickly as possible back to following instructions toward despair. What is wonderful about my hope is that she chose to be different, to be less dull and more flamboyant, to be wiser than the way laid out for most women and men to be. She is evidence that the rest of us can become ourselves as well.

When I say that I want to demonstrate the power of small places over big systems, I have to be careful not to be a jerk about it. Big systems are going to continue to have power, and many lunches I will not even be able to keep my children from spilling their milk. The power of these small-storied places is not to make things perfect; rather, their power is in allowing life to matter. Their power is in taking away the helplessness, the "we seemed to ourselves as grasshoppers" feeling that the Book of Numbers made so famous (*Numbers 13.33*). Much of what is wrong with life is life-derived, or human-derived, not systems-derived. It is very important to retain the capacity to distinguish between systems-derived garbage and stuff that just seems to be there, rooted deep in the contrariness of things.

For example, many people keep trying to find their way back home, back to a simpler place, a more child-like place. All the way home, we hum the tune, "You can't go home again," but we keep putting one foot in front of the other anyway. It's a good thing about us humans that while seriously complicating our existence, we are also hell bent on simplifying it. It's one of the contrary strains and one of those things that we really can't blame the systems for.

The standard problems of a woman's safety while alone and traveling is a perfect example. Everyone has a point of view on the subject. But the other dangers, of traveling together and staying home, are much more serious. And about these, few have given much thought.

One danger while traveling is not finding what you are looking for. Another is disappointment at what you see. A third is the discovery that life elsewhere is pretty much the same as it is back home. Travel will prove as nothing else can that a central ambiguity women face is the longing to be at home while away and the longing to be away while at home. This doubleness is a surprise only to the fainthearted; to those who understand the powers of storied places, it is simply confirmation. There are enormous similarities between home and away, in and out, even if we don't have to make our own bed or do our own dishes.

The best trip I ever took was in my home town. It was the plunge in divinity school. With an allotment of five dollars and a story of borrowed identity, we traveled Chicago for three days, experiencing life as a person down and out. The second and third best travel experiences were touring with youth groups in New York and San Francisco, eating at the soup kitchens, sleeping on the floors, and keeping our eyes open. We called these trips urban exposures and they were, yielding more knowledge about home than we could imagine. We gathered a perspective from which to see home that we didn't have before.

The worst trip I ever took was in search of female history. I can't tell you how glad I am that the photographs of the historical marker at Seneca Falls Women's Rights Convention didn't turn out. The reason is that the marker stands on the site of the Seneca Falls laundromat. While I thought it humorous that day, back home it would have depressed me. A trip earlier that same day to the Oneida community had nearly left me in tears. On the site of this experiment in communal living stands nothing less than the flashy Oneida Silver Company, an alternative to absolutely nothing. In an unparalleled historical compensation, Oneida is notorious for making money off wedding gifts. Even their ads ooze monogamous bliss as though no one had ever said anything at Oneida about the limitations of monogamy. When asked if there was anything socialist about the earlier community, our guide took out her smelling salts. The history I had been seeking was forgotten at Oneida, washed away at Seneca Falls. You can't really blame big systems for the amnesia of local communities. You really have to blame local communities.

Travel instructs that all the difference you need is right in your home town, while at the same time amply demonstrating that other people's home towns are as adept as yours at forgetting identity.

The disappointments of travel do not mean that home satisfies. So I travel to find another table, longing for and rueing the one back home; to sleep in another bed, knowing that what spine I have is sheltered in that bed I have made and have to make. Another way of saying all this is to say that moving around will neither get rid of or add to the trouble of living in a wrongly systematized world or under the existential contraries.

Too much thought goes into the dangers and the possibilities of travel. This implies that we are safe at home, which we are not. Danger travels too. The only safety is in eyes that remain open to exposure to double longings: when at home, to travel and when traveling, to be at home. Security requires many selves and many stories, visits to all the storied places, many found by traveling but mostly realized by staying home.

If traveling is one of the places where messages mix it up with each other, so is writing. These features of our ordinary lives carry the contrariness, which is beyond the reach of big systems. Systems make it more difficult to understand their mix, but the mix will be there even after we stop taking orders from the captains.

I would never have given writing a second thought if it hadn't been for Mrs. O'Shea, my English teacher in the tenth grade. She wrote "superlative" on one of my essays and that was that. From then on, I kept writing just to see that word once more. I don't know when habit replaced the search for praise. I do know that upward mobility's tentacles reach into my writing; I lose a lot of pleasure to performance and publishing. But writing without the dollar attached to it is still possible; it is just as difficult as writing with the dollar attached.

I write to clarify, to see what is so, and what isn't. I write to discover what I think and why I think it. I write to give the big systems a run for their money. I write to see what I know that I don't know I know. The complications are extraordinary, the lying intense.

I write in Chinese restaurants before the soup comes. I write during dull meetings. I wake up at six a.m. for months to finish a long project before my children awake and contribute the confusion my writing clarifies. I make notes on menus, business cards, checks, and receipts. I really can't stop thinking about writing because it is there that I will clarify what matters and what doesn't.

So painfully is much of the time given over to the unimportant that writing is almost sheer pleasure. We have to scrap with the big systems to be able to use our time well, but even after the scrap, we then have the task of using the time we had given away and now have taken back. It is amazing how the clock keeps ticking through the writing process. How to find the time to write, how to use it well once we have found it, are serious issues for a writer. I never knew one who wasn't talking about time.

Is this because writers are hooked on production, hooked on the money and the mobility that comes from completed projects? Or is it because we are so hungry for meaning that we particularly abhor wiping up spills, and looking for our missing keys, and putting gas in the car, and standing in line at the grocery? Do we imagine ourselves better than these enterprises? A similar question could be asked of any go-getter. Why hurry if grace abounds? Why worry if all value is already given to all people by a loving God?

In the answer to this question about pace and clock, the mixture is revealed. We are each a partner to the big systems, and we are each a partner of smaller places. We have possibilities and we are captive. We follow orders and we resist. The mixture of motives at any given moment makes us who we are. But there is always a mixture. Nobody is free of the systems' orders to move quickly, not even the artist, not even the fully faithful. To think otherwise about systems, to assume that individually we can get beyond them or through them or not discover them in our bath water, is to be a jerk about it. After the revolution, or redemption, or whatever it will be, even when the big systems have been as deflated as most of us now are, we will still find ourselves troubled about how and where to go. Perfection is not our destination so much as freedom to enjoy the places in which we find ourselves. Sometimes hurrying is a way to enjoy a place, sometimes it is an affront.

I go through weeks vowing to improve my word-processing skills to manage better the production of my scratchy words. Or, on the other extreme, I'll buy linen paper and only use a Mont Blanc pen on it. New posies on a well-dusted table, skylights installed over it, or other environmental considerations gobble up enormous amounts of time. Actually I write best when the writing takes over and I stop pursuing efficiency. I write best when my kids are coloring Mickey Mouse feet with a well-interrogated orange, and spilling grape juice, and demanding snaps on their pocketbooks. At these times, a Bic pen and a refrigerator magnet pad will do for a paragraph or two. Assuming, of course, I have located some meaning that matters. Or a funny story. Or some new perspective on an old place.

The sermons always come like this. After carrying the text around in my subconscious all week, I get to Saturday when I must find the beginning that predicts the end and fill in the middle. That interesting notion of the DNA all residing in the first sentence compares quite well to the folk wisdom that everyone already has their appointment with death. Start labor when the baby is ready to come, and stop it when the genes are spent. Have fun in the middle, remembering the beginning, heading firmly toward the end; if you wander, double back. Try to remember that it is more important that the Word of God be spoken than that you get positives after the service. Offend if you must, but include yourself in the accusation.

The sermons ritualize the week. They allow the time to come out right. Some people tell me that church is like this for them too. Once, for four years, I had a job teaching ministry rather than doing it. I didn't preach every Sunday, so I had a lot of unused material. I got depressed every Saturday night because I had stories but no one to listen to them. It reminded me of feelings I have when I discover my friends don't compost. What a terrible waste.

My husband, alert to these compulsions, is always warning me to leave him out of it. When an interesting or difficult thing happens, I'm glad because I see the story in it. He fears even more publicity to what he used to call his private life. He remains miffed about a certain sermon that features suspenders. The children are still too young to know that their school buses were just on the radio or that their misnomers make great illustrations. My problem is worrying what others do when their car breaks down on the way to a beach vacation, and no part can be located until the day after the vacation would have ended if you had gotten there. Where do people put woe they can't compost? How else can you fight big systems except with stories, except by breaking the silence of confidentiality about things that hurt us? How else can you get a big system's goat if you don't tell stories and distinguish the system-caused problem and the problem that came with the bath water?

I believe in spreading trouble around, not hiding it. That's why every request I get for confidentiality is denied. Just don't tell me, I'll say. The reason is once I heard a whale of a story about a priest abusing a parishioner. I had promised confidentiality. It was a mistake. The sooner small place people discover how much we have in common, the sooner we will stop using the captain's words and come up with some of our own.

Telling the stories doesn't mean I don't have ulcers. I am not without hiding places. I can't really find words for most of what goes on. Sometimes you just had to be there, if you know what I mean. Simply, much of what others would toss, I tell. The days when my essays were graded are long gone. Now I have readers and listeners, not teachers, to please.

My finest praise comes from my Christmas card list. Every year the project I work on the hardest is that Christmas letter. Once I began being published, and feeling quite self-important about that superlative, I found it more difficult to write for a strictly personal audience. The embarrassment in that mixture gave all of Novembers to the Christmas letter. This way that writing for money and by-lines has of replacing writing for friends and fun shames me. Which is why I penitentially make such a project out of our church newsletter or thank-you notes. Imagine. My beginning as a writer was to seek praise; I press on to avoid shame.

Another mixture. Exactly the same issue as men: We can't live with them and we can't live without them. Home and away, praise and shame, hope in high-heeled sneakers. No, things do not want to tidy up. They want to stay messy, even with the systemic wolves outside of every door. After the revolution and redemption, when the big systems are brought down and the valleys exalted, these mixes will continue. The tidy parts of ourselves well acquainted with storied places will feel right at home in the contrariness. We will not be surprised at lions living so close to lambs. The helplessness will continue, but at least it will be our own. We won't be able to blame it on the captain anymore.

I'll never forget the day we moved from Chicago to New York. Getting the moving van packed with three kids under four underfoot was a realistic impersonation of hell. The heat. The dirt. The endless cleaning. Exhaustion all the way to the fingernails. Much guilt about moving again after so many moves. Much fear that New York would be just another way station on the endless, absurd search for happiness that adulthood had become. Real conflict about the ordained ministry of parish versus the political possibilities of a more regional, ecumenical position. In brief, a ditch of a day. We left Chicago only to have the energy for a two hour drive. We found a motel and checked in. We tried to watch the television, but all kind of sat in a daze, batting flies, and wishing we were dead. Finally the kids went to sleep and a few hours later, Isaac, the eldest, woke up screaming. A heartwrenching scream. "Home!" he yelled, "I want to go home. I don't want to go to New York. I want to go home to Chicago."

In the middle of my journey, in the middle of the woods, I lost my way. So wrote Dante in _The Divine Comedy_. I didn't know how to console that child. I had to uproot him. It was the best mixed decision for all of us. But, imagine, having to cause pain to your baby because you have to cease pain to yourself, because you have to find what you're looking for, even if you don't know where it is. Imagine. We can't even really protect our own children from harm or hurt.

Now, lots of people use these kinds of realities to protect themselves from the pain of big systems and their participation in that pain. It used to be good, but now it isn't. Or, (the past can be used in so many ways) it was always this bad. Even, they will say, if we blunt big systems, there will still be sickness, and anxiety, and rushing, and impure motives and children crying. Let's go hide in a glorious past, or a glorious future, or anywhere but here, anything but now. There is no way out of the contrariness of wanting to be home while traveling, and wanting to travel while home.

Yes, we will have to say, good and bad have every intention of mixing it up with each other. Small places see this every day, all the time. We see the mixtures, we report the mixtures, we actually enjoy the mixtures. We just see no reason to add to the down side, to add to the insult of bad health and brother-in-laws, the oppression of sexism, or racism, or poverty, or violence. We see no reason why, with aging being as hard as it already is, we should consent to the further indignity of seeing ourselves as irrelevant or useless. We live in a place, don't we? We have stories to tell, don't we? What's the problem if economic systems have or find no use for us? We have use for each other. Why should congregations and communities, which could be such sources of solace and gladness, be relegated to following the captain's orders? Why should they take their instructions from upward mobility or psychologized language or management strategies? Why should we give our powers away just because some big system captain wants us to?

When big systems are put in their place, small places will become the systems by which we live. Their system is story. The strategy to get from here, where we are dominated by big system instructions, to there, where we will be free of such instructions to mix it up our own way, the strategy is also story. Break the silence, speak, tell how it is where we are. We will get there by going there and discover at the end of the storied journey that we have been there all along.

Maybe our home will be in the middle of our journey, in the middle of the wood, a fire built, fellow travelers gathered around, telling stories.

bibliography

Alinsky, Saul. *Rules for Radicals*. New York: Random House. 1971.

Alsop, Susan Mary. *Lady Sackville: A Biography*. New York: Doubleday & Co. 1978.

Bellah, Robert. *Habits of the Heart*. Berkeley: University of California Press. 1985.

Briand, Jr., Paul. *Daughter of the Sky: The Story of Amelia Earhart*. New York: Duell, Sloan, and Pearce. 1960.

Dante, Alighieri. *The Divine Comedy*. New York: Norton. 1977.

de Beauvoir, Simone. *The Second Sex*. New York: Knopf. 1968.

Goldman, Emma. *Living My Life*. New York: New American Library. 1977.

Griffith, Elisabeth. *In Her Own Right: The Life of Elizabeth Cady Stanton*. New York: Oxford University Press. 1984.

Hill, Mary A. *Charlotte Perkins Gilman: The Making of a Radical Feminist, 1860–1896*. Philadelphia: Temple University Press. 1980.

James, Henry. *The Bostonians*. New York: New American Library. 1979.

Lerner, Michael, ed. *Tikkun*. Institute of Labor and Mental Health. (March, April 1988).

Lewis, R.W.B. *Edith Wharton: A Biography*. New York: Harper & Row. 1975.

Olsen, Tillie. *Yorrondio: From the Thirties*. New York: Delacorte. 1974.

Plath, Sylvia. *The Bell Jar*. New York: Bantam Books. 1981.

Sarton, May. *Journal of a Solitude*. New York: Norton. 1973.

Schaef, Anne Wilson. *Women's Reality: An Emerging Female System in the White Male Society*. New York: Harper & Row. 1986.

Shulman, Alix, ed. *Red Emma Speaks: Selected Writings and Speeches*. New York: Random House. 1972.

Thoreau, Henry David. *A Week on the Concord and Merrimack Rivers*. New York: New American Library. 1961.

Thurber, James. *My Life and Hard Times*. New York: Harper & Row. 1933.

Wharton, Edith. *The Reef*. New York: Scribner. 1965.

THE AUTHOR: Donna Schaper

Donna Schaper is the pastor of the First Congregational Church in Riverhead, New York. She was born near the Hudson River. She teaches a little, organizes a little, travels around a little, and has as her destination the Renaissance woman. She has a Renaissance husband, three children, a striped cat, a golden dog, four red chickens, and a very hot compost pile that shelters thousands of worms. Walking, gardening, and friends are her chief sources of pleasure, rivaling only the gladness she experiences when small places and small people give big systems the shake.

the
WOMEN's
series

LURAMEDIA presents

The hallmark of The Women's Series is honest and lively writing that articulates the full range of women's experiences. Our dream is to publish short books or tapes in many forms — poetry, dialogues, monologues, journaling excerpts, personal stories, letters — that will speak woman-to-woman across space and time. We want women to hear these voices, feel comforted and challenged, because they, too, have felt the same emotions and seen the same visions.

THE WOMEN'S SERIES includes...

Superwoman Turns 40 by Donna Schaper
  The story of one woman's intentions to grow up. For women turning around in the middle of life and coming home to themselves. Celebrates the small gifts of caring in the midst of life's chaotic demands.
    (ISBN 0-931055-67-1)

River of Promise by Judy Dahl
  An unusual story of love and adoption. For all those engaged in the struggles and joys of raising children in a nontraditional family. Speaks with warmth and compassion to the issue of adoption by single and homosexual parents.
    (ISBN 0-931055-64-4)

Circle of Stones by Judith Duerk
  A collection of reflections, imagery, and stories for women who are rediscovering their identity. Emphasizes the importance of letting one's unique spirit come to birth and attending to the inner voice.
    (ISBN 0-931055-66-0)

LuraMedia Publications

by Marjory Zoet Bankson
BRAIDED STREAMS
Esther and a Woman's Way
of Growing
(ISBN 0-931055-05-09)

SEASONS OF FRIENDSHIP
Naomi and Ruth
as a Pattern
(ISBN 0-931055-41-5)

by Alla Renée Bozarth
WOMANPRIEST
A Personal Odyssey
(ISBN 0-931055-51-2)

by Lura Jane Geiger
ASTONISH ME, YAHWEH!
Leader's Guide
(ISBN 0-931055-02-4)

by Lura Jane Geiger
and Patricia Backman
BRAIDED STREAMS
Leader's Guide
(ISBN 0-931055-09-1)

by Lura Jane Geiger, Sandy Landstedt,
Mary Geckeler, and Peggy Oury
ASTONISH ME, YAHWEH!
A Bible Workbook-Journal
(ISBN 0-931055-01-6)

by Kenneth L. Gibble
THE GROACHER FILE
A Satirical Exposé of
Detours to Faith
(ISBN 0-931055-55-5)

by Ronna Fay Jevne, Ph.D.
and Alexander Levitan, M.D.
NO TIME FOR NONSENSE
Self-Help for the Seriously Ill
(ISBN 0-931055-63-6)

by Ted Loder
EAVESDROPPING ON THE ECHOES
Voices from the Old Testament
(ISBN 0-931055-42-3 HB)
(ISBN 0-931055-58-X PB)

GUERRILLAS OF GRACE
Prayers for the Battle
(ISBN 0-931055-01-6)

NO ONE BUT US
Personal Reflections on
Public Sanctuary
(ISBN 0-931055-08-3)

TRACKS IN THE STRAW
Tales Spun from the Manger
(ISBN 0-931055-06-7)

by Jacqueline McMakin
with Sonya Dyer
WORKING FROM THE HEART
For Those Who Hunger for Meaning
and Satisfaction in Their Work
(ISBN 0-931055-65-2)

by Elizabeth O'Connor
SEARCH FOR SILENCE
Revised Edition
(ISBN 0-931055-07-5)

by Donna Schaper
BOOK OF COMMON POWER
Narratives Against the Current
(ISBN 0-931055-67-9)

by Renita Weems
JUST A SISTER AWAY
A Womanist Vision of Women's
Relationships in the Bible
(ISBN 0-931055-52-0)

LuraMedia is a company that searches for ways to encourage personal growth, shares the excitement of creative integrity, and believes in the power of faith to change lives.